Longboarder's Start-Up

A

The
Bush/
rized
in or
as the

Longboarder's Start-Up:
A Guide to Longboard Surfing
By Doug Werner

Published by:
Tracks Publishing
140 Brightwood Avenue
Chula Vista, CA 91910
(619) 476-7125

Publisher's Cataloging in Publication

Werner, Doug, 1950-
    Longboarder's start-up : a guide to longboard surfing / Doug Werner
    p. cm. – (Start-up sports ; #6)
    Includes bibliographical references and index.
    LCCN: 96-60497
    ISBN: 1-884654-06-1

    1. Surfing.   I. Title.   II. Series.

GV840.S8W37 1996   797.3'2
                                    QBI96-20419

Dedicated

to

Dad

EP "Red" Werner

Acknowledgements:

Stewart Surfboards
Bill Stewart
Henry Ford
Professional Longboard Association
Rita Bohanan
Bob Bohanan
Colin McPhillips
Ted Robinson
Mark Stewart
Kathleen Wheeler
Dan Mann
Jay Novak
Christine Gillard
Mike Gillard
Mark Suchomel
Mark Noble
Larry Block
Todd Huber
Dan Domancich
Leon Chow
Robin Niehaus
Stu Kenson
Paulo Cabral
Josh Baxter
Joel Tudor
Katie Ryan
Beth Engel
Geoff "Red" Whisner
Lynn's Photo

Preface

Design innovations and a new appreciation for the grace and poise of surfing a longer board has lifted the art of longboarding back into the limelight and, more importantly, *back into the minds* of serious surfers who want to expand their wave riding experience.

Longboarder's Start-Up is a guide for surfing beginners as well as practicing shortboarders who have never tried to longboard. We tried to keep stuff easy to follow and (at least for a textbook) fun to read, too.

The book has two parts. The first half covers equipment and surfing basics through standing up. Although alot of this is for beginners, veteran shortboard surfers should read the chapter on equipment and those sections in each chapter that deal with their concerns about wave selection, trimming, courtesy and taking off. An expert shortboarder may think he knows it all, but there are a few differences between shortboarding and longboarding basics that should be noted.

The second part gets into traditional longboard technique and a step or two beyond. Beginning with the craft of cross-stepping and trimming, we cover turning and turning maneuvers, essential noseriding and finally, some of the tricks that the pros execute so flawlessly.

All the key points are brought home with scads of

photos and a stripped down text that is totally void of the mall surfer lingo that has mysteriously mucked-up surfing's image since 1962 *(But dude!)*

Nothing, of course, replaces learning by doing. But *Longboarder's Start-Up* is designed and written to be a heck of a good start for just about anybody. There's information here that you'll find nowhere else. And it will help. Guaranteed.

So good luck and have fun. Respect the ocean, the sport, and the surfers who came before you as well as yourself.

It all comes around.

Doug Werner
Tracks

Contents

The Essence of Longboarding is Style: Although the evolution of surfboard design has provided today's longboard surfer with vehicles that can rip, slash and burn like never before, the classic core remains the same. Above, Henry Ford displays some vintage style and a terrific set of abs in this photo from 1963. Below and three decades later, Ted Robinson nonchalantly rips the top off.

1   **2**

Trends

Until the 50s, surfboards were *very* big, *very* heavy and *very* long. Also very wooden. Those early redwood and/or balsa monsters measured up to 15 feet and sometimes weighed over 100 pounds. Obviously, being hard core, or committed, had a whole new meaning back in 1951.

The advent of fiberglass and foam construction in 1958 gave surfers a lighter, more maneuverable vehicle to ride, but for another ten years or so boards were still around ten feet long.

That all changed in the late 60s.

Surfers discovered that they could successfully ride surfboards much shorter and lighter than previously thought. With less weight and a tighter turning radius, the shorter boards enabled surfers to execute dramatic directional changes that were impossible on a longboard. They could also fit into places that the longer boards couldn't, resulting in new levels of tuberiding theatrics in particular.

The drawn out lines of longboarding gave way to the slashing, lip-smashing, tube-hugging style of modern shortboard surfing. Almost overnight all the standard guides that had determined surfboard size according to height and weight were tossed. An era of experimentation with no limits had begun.

For 20 years the world's lineups were almost exclusively owned by shortboarders. Longboards were like elevator music. Only kooks and cranky old men surfed logs, ie, the dinged and shapeless barges that most longboards were before 1990. In 1982 you'd spot an Edsel next to you in the water before you'd see a longboard.

Then the 90s meandered into our lives:

1) We Got Older

Surfing became multi-generational. Surfers got older like alotta people do and all of a sudden longboards were OK because the longboarding riding style became more suitable to the growing numbers of mid-life riders.

2) They Came Back

Former surfers who took a break from the beach to build careers and families began coming back to the sport in droves. Their board of choice was longish because that's what they remembered.

3) From Kook to Classic

A new appreciation for the grace (and glory) of longboardsmanship changed the image of longboarding from kooky to classic. Longboarding became a class-act and the classic essence of the surfing lifestyle.

4) Hot Sticks, Hot Surfers, High Performance!

And perhaps most importantly, all of those wonderful design innovations started showing up in the new longboards. Just like *that* longboards weren't logs anymore. They became very cool things to ride because they could *turn*.

1

2

3

4

5

The Julliard School of Longboarding: Mark Stewart's classy display in this sequence shows off both the dance-like quality of top-notch longboarding and the high performance capabilities of today's modern longboard.

Noseriding: The quintessential longboarding maneuver.

No Kidding: Smacking the lip with a longboard is just as much fun as hitting it with your shortboard.

Longboards became *High Performance Vehicles.*

So good surfers started riding them and they *ripped.* Which turned on everybody watching them. Finally, all the watchers became tryers. The tryers were not only the greyheads, but the kids, too. The real hot kids.

Until there you have it:

The Second Coming of Longboarding.

Here to Stay

Surfing will not turn its back on longboarding again like it did in the 70s and 80s. Shortboarding will continue to dominate because of its sheer versatility, but the sport and the lifestyle are big enough and old enough now to absorb longboarding as a very legitimate and equally satisfying way to ride waves.

It's a great way to expand your surfing horizons because there's stuff you can do on a longboard that you just can't do on a shortboard:

1) Walking the Walk

The simple act of trimming with the cross-step is exhilarating when successfully executed. Gaining proficiency will make you feel like a Bruce Lee or a Gene Kelly, depending on the wave and your frame of mind.

2) Toes on the Nose

Noseriding is noseriding, of course. It's the only way a surfer can ride a wave without anything sticking out in front. Many have likened it to surfing without a surfboard.

3) Surf Anything

And longboards can handle the mushiest or tiniest waves and flattest sections with ease.

4) It's Really Cool

Moreover, it just *feels* different to ride a nine foot board. And that difference is really cool in almost any kind of surf, no matter what you're doing. Just taking off,

Surfing One Foot Slop and Loving It:

On a miserable day for surfing in general, and shortboarding in particular, Ted Robinson still gets a fun little ride on his longboard. The greater planing surface of a longboard enables surfers to ride even the smallest mush with ease. And, in Ted's case, with a whole lotta style.

(In sequence from left to right)

turning, bouncing off a section, or whatever is alotta fun because it's a wonderful new way to enjoy the riding experience.

And just in case you were thinking that I was going to wax poetic or profound... all this longboarding business, like everything else about surfing in general or particular, is about having fun. Or should be at any rate.

So there. Have some.

Welcome to Longboard Surfing.

Study in Speed: Mark Stewart contemplates a trip through the piling during a contest at Huntington Beach, California.

Part One:

- Equipment

- Waves

- Pop-Ups

- Paddling

- Rules

- Safety

- Punching Through & Diving Under

- Catching Waves

Tight Radius:
Colin Mcphillips whips his shortboard into a tight turn as soon as he *wills* it.

→

1

Wider Radius (But Just as Cool):
Colin makes a similar directional change on his longboard which requires a bit more preparation and a lot more room to execute due to the increased length and turning radius of his 9' surfboard.

2

The Long and Short of It

In general, a surfboard is considered a shortboard if it measures no more than seven feet or so in length. It's considered a longboard if it measures nine feet or longer. A board that measures between eight and nine feet is often called a funboard, but that's really just another name for a longboard on the short side. Because anything over eight feet will probably *ride* like a longboard. Meaning that the surfer must move fore and aft in order to maintain trim during the course of a ride.

By and large, a surfer can remain in one spot on a shortboard. Most changes in trim and/or direction are made with weight shifts.

So it's the length of the board that determines the style of riding. Longboarding requires stepping and weight shifts, shortboarding requires mostly weight shifts, with very little footwork.

Since the turning radius on a longboard is so much greater than a shortboard, maneuvers on a longboard are more drawn out. It takes more time and effort to swing all that board length around. And the length limits where the board can fit and go on the wave.

Longboard surfing often has a *swooping* look and feel to it. The rider seems to be performing a dance or a martial arts exercise while riding. All that swooping and dancing can make for a very graceful display with an experienced rider.

The best ones make it look like Art.

In stark contrast, shortboards are made to *whip* about in tight turns and ride in tight places. Surfer, surfboard and wave can meld as one during a ride, slashing back and forth, up and down. Expert shortboarders appear to *hurtle* with the wave in one careening maneuver after another. The pure athleticism among the world's best shortboard surfers is as breathtaking as any in all of sport.

Michael Jordan has nothing on Kelly Slater.

The Surfboard

There is alot to choose from these days. Surfboards come in various lengths, thicknesses, shapes, and fin arrangements. Surfboards are not mass produced and popped out of some mold. Each is hand shaped and, as such, inherently unique. It's one of the reasons why surfing isn't a sport on the scale of in-line skating, basketball, or even snowboarding. Surfboard manufacturing is an intensely individualistic and personal endeavor that keeps the Real Big Boys out of the game. The heart and soul of the industry remains in the hands of highly talented craftsmen who have learned their shaping skills from creating and personally surfing countless wave riding vehicles.

Although surfboard design is right up there with NASA and cutting edge computer technology, materials and manufacturing haven't changed much since 1958 when Hobie Alter and Gordon Clark came up with the first urethane blank, or foam core, for a surfboard. The foam core is reinforced with wood stringers that run the middle length of the board, hand shaped with planing and sanding devices, then sealed with fiberglass and resin.

Here are some basic elements:

Length-- As surfboards get longer, the influence of edges, or rails, become greater and must be taken into account before any change of direction is considered while riding. Shortboards can be flicked almost at will because the amount of rail involved with the wave at any one time is so small. Longboard rails set a track in the wave. They, along with the fins, determine direction.

Also, the longer the board, the greater the glide. As surface area increases, surfboards become easier and faster to paddle. They pick up waves sooner, ride faster and are able to sustain momentum through the flatter areas of a wave.

Rails-- Rounder, more full rails tend to push water and reduce a board's ability to turn and gain speed. As the rail is turned down to form a harder edge, a board can be released from its track more easily, resulting in quicker, tighter turns and increased acceleration.

Outline-- If you were to trace around a surfboard lying upon the sand, you would be tracing that board's outline. Surfboards with wide and curvy tails are easier to turn and are turned further back than boards with straight and narrow tails. Boards with straight and narrow tails are designed for bigger surf and need alotta speed to turn properly. At slower speeds they tend to track, or dig their rails when a rider attempts to turn.

Outline: In this view you can clearly see the outline of the surfboard shape. The more the outline curves out, the easier it is to turn. As the outline straightens and the sides become more parallel, the board becomes faster and less capable of turning.

Models: Beth Engel & Katie Ryan

Rocker: Surfboards aren't completely flat. Each has a kick along its length or in specific areas to achieve different results. For example, a kicked tail helps a board to noseride and turn. A kicked nose enables a board to maneuver vertically and helps prevent pearling (nosediving).

Rocker-- The flatter the board, the faster it goes. The more bend or *rocker* a board has, the easier it is to maneuver. Different degrees of rocker can be shaped into different areas of the board to achieve specific results. For example, boards designed for noseriding have a pronounced rocker in the tail that flattens out towards the nose. Boards designed for vertical surfing (off-the-lips, floaters, etc.) have heavily rockered tails for quick turns as well as lifted noses to prevent pearling.

Fins-- Fins function as pivot points and stabilizers during directional changes. A traditional large, single fin arrangement provides stability. Tri-fins hold the rails in the wave and enable the rider to pump his board rail to rail to gain quick acceleration and to execute power turns without spinning out. Small dual-fin arrangements rely on an expert surfer's ability to use the rails to control his turning.

Thickness-- In general, fatter boards float better than thinner boards. Of course, thick and thin can be shaped into the same board. For example, a board may be thin in the nose, tail and/or rails, yet thick in the middle.

Weight-- Weight is determined by a number of things: foam density, length, layers of fiberglass and resin, stringers and width. Heavy boards are stronger, yet less maneuverable than lighter boards.

Width-- Wider boards are more stable, while narrow boards yield quicker directional changes. Like thickness, wide and narrow can be incorporated into the same design and the middle measurement is the most important measurement.

Thickness and Rails: Thicker boards float better than thinner ones, but are less maneuverable. All rails used to be big and fat. They pushed water and made turning difficult. Rails on today's high performance longboards are turned down to meet the flats of the bottom of the board. A harder edge is shaped around the tail to "release" water and gain speed. Rails are tucked and foiled to "hold" water and prevent spinning out.

Fins and Tail Designs: As much as anything else, advances in fin and tail designs have made longboarding a high performance pursuit. The tri-fin arrangement was first designed into a longboard by Bill Stewart in 1984. Tri-fins enable longboarders to pump rail to rail from the back of their boards much like shortboarders do in order to gain quick acceleration. Three fins also enable surfers to noseride low in the face of the wave and make sideslipping and 360 maneuvers easier to learn and execute.

The Board for You

Beginners should opt for a nine-foot board or there-abouts, with either a normal single- or tri-fin arrangement. The outline should be somewhat curvy and the rocker average. Thick and wide is good for stability. It's nice to get a heavier seal of glass and resin because the board will last longer, however, this will also make the board heavier.

Stay away from narrow and thin because they'll be very difficult to even sit on properly, let alone stand.

As you progress, you'll develop your own style and preferences. You should start and maintain relationships with shapers who surf the same spots as you and know how you surf. That way the surfboard shapes that you buy can develop with your surfing.

If you're crossing-over from shortboarding, you'll want a higher performance design that will allow you to still surf with alotta the speed, acceleration and turning capabilities that you enjoyed as a shortboarder (no, you don't have to give them up!). That'll probably mean three fins, hard-edged rails, a thinner, narrower shape and a rockered out nose.

But in the end it's all preference. And finding a shaper who will work with your needs. Be honest about your skill level and find something that works for you as opposed to keeping up with the latest trend.

Wetsuit, Leash & Wax

Outside of the tropics you'll need a wetsuit. The cheaper ones fall apart. Buy a leading brand with quality double stitching and sealed seams. Cold water requires 2 or 3 millimeters of thickness, or some combination thereof. Very cold water requires at least 3 millimeters and may require more.

Leashes are a must for most of us. Get one that will last.

Wax is the stuff you rub on the top of the board to prevent slipping. The best wax rubs on in perfect little beads. A comb-like gizmo, called, oddly enough, the wax comb, is used to furrow and roughen old and slick wax already on the board.

Basic Tool

It's very easy to get into surfboard design. It's only natural to want to keep up with the latest thing. And it's always so great to get a brand new board from a talented shaper.

But one of the most moving surfing photographs I've ever seen shows a guy surfing a door. That's right, a door. And it looks like a pretty good ride, too. The wave's hot, the rider's in the slot, and the water is a perfect emerald green. The surfer is obviously without means in a third world country that probably doesn't even have a surf shop. Chances are he has never even seen a modern surfboard.

But there he is... surfing. Maybe not exactly like the rest of us on our signature models, but surfing, and having a great time doing it, just the same.

That picture tells me everything I need to remember about why I surf. Looking a little farther beyond the glossy thrill of owning a slick new stick is the utter joy of just being able to ride waves.

For many of us not a whole lot more even matters.

For an in-depth review of surfboard design please refer to the interview with Bill Stewart and Henry Ford beginning on page 119.

Chapter Two

Surfable Waves

Not all waves are surfable. As a surfable line of swell reaches the shallows along a given stretch of coastline, it begins to rear up and break at one point along its length. Then from that initial point it continues to pitch in a gradual manner in either one or two directions, depending on the geography of the area. A gradual break provides the surfer with a moving wall of unbroken wave surface upon which to angle away from the breaking part of the wave, or curl.

Waves that break all at once along their length are called close outs and do not allow the surfer to angle. All one can do is ride straight ahead with the surging white water. Although this is a part of surfing, riding the soup really ain't where it's at because it's just a bumpy, boring journey into the sand or rocks. Racing ahead of, or under the pitching peak provides the real thrill. The essence of surfing is located along the line of ledging swell that stretches out ahead like a perfect peeling highway.

Surfable Wave: Note how this wave is breaking uniformly from right to left, providing the surfer with a clean shoulder to ride.This powerful, well-shaped wave is perfect for longboarding. (So where is everybody?)

Closed Out Wave: Instead of a clear path, this surfer is facing a wall breaking along its entire length.There's no place to go except straight in with the white water.

Small and Mushy: A typical beach break just this side of being blown out. Still, the waves are well-formed and breaking softly down their faces. Easily longboardable.

Overhead with a 1/2 break: Mike Gillard's wave is larger and more powerful than the surf pictured above. The lip is pitching about halfway down the face. Still very longboardable although getting out is a little more work.

Surf spots can be roughly categorized as beach breaks, reef breaks and point breaks:

Beach breaks are sand bottomed and depend on the shifting moods of sandbars to provide the mold for the shape of the swells that arrive. Because sandbars are changing things, so are the shapes of the waves that break over them. Waves begin to break over the shallow areas of the bottom and peel towards the deeper water at either or both ends of the particular sandbar.

Reef breaks have beds of rocks, rock formations and/or coral that shape the bottom. These breaks are usually more consistent than beach breaks because the bottoms are literally rock solid. The waves break over the highest levels of the reef first and taper in one or two directions towards the deeper water.

Point breaks provide a jutting point of land to influence the lines of swell that sweep towards it. As the lines arrive they wrap themselves around the point and conform to the special land and bottom formations. As each line gradually reaches the shallow water, one end touching before the other, the swell begins to break and peel in a perfect sweep as the rest of the line catches up to meet the shallows.

Longboardable Waves

The Kind

Size isn't as critical as many think. Shape, or wave type, plays the most critical role.

Waves can be generally categorized or typed simply by the way they spill over or break. If the breaking part of the wave forms a lip and pitches out, around and down– all the way down to the trough or base of the wave– the wave is said to be top-to-bottom. This is also called a barrel or a tube.

Top-to-bottom waves break hard and have power at any size. The inherent steepness of top-to-bottom waves make riding longboards a little tricky because things get tight real quick. Longboards just don't fit or react well in waves where the bottom literally drops out. There's alotta board to maneuver in very little time.

Not to say that you cannot ride barrels on a longboard, but late take offs are tough to make in hard breaking surf. Longboards, being long, can't squirt out of a ledge situation very well. You need to catch the wave early. And don't expect to tuck into the tube as easily as you can on a shortboard.

Wipe outs in hollow surf can be murder. Unlike shortboards, longboards don't always bob away from your body when you get hammered. Hugging a nine foot stick in the slammer is brutal.

As waves get less steep and hollow, they become more suitable for the larger planing surface of a longboard. And in many cases, less suitable for the smaller planing surface of a shortboard. Actually, shortboards thrive on steep breaking sections because they need speed to keep them afloat and moving. Less steep or mushy waves don't always provide enough speed to keep a short stick on track. Of course shortboards can react sooner to the lickity-split action of a hollow wave and they fit inside the roaring hole a heck of a lot easier than a longboard.

Longboards thrive on mushburgers big and small. They get into the wave better and easier during take offs and negotiate the flat or slow sections with ease. On a smaller board a surfer has to jump and pump in order to make it through the dead spots.

Of course, the real tiny stuff is for longboards only. One-foot mush can't really push a shortboard enough. And if you can't get up and going during the take off, you ain't going. Longboards have more surface to pick up the swell and can sorta glide into wave conditions that are almost non-existent.

Not Really the Kind

Once you're an accomplished longboard surfer you can surf almost anywhere. After all, surfing is surfing. But there are conditions more and less suitable for a longer surfboard.

Before you can surf a wave you have to paddle out to where the waves break, or the lineup.

You can't dive under a broken wave (duck dive) with your longboard as easily as you can with a shortboard. Although it is possible to duck dive with a longer board, it takes a good deal more effort. So paddling out on big, hard breaking days can be very difficult and tiring. Especially at beach breaks where there are no lulls or flat spots in the impact zone.

Getting out in those conditions is sometimes impossible. And even if you make it once, there's no certainty that you'll make it again after a ride. Of course the beating that you'll take trying will render you a broken, exhausted and crying-for-mama mess.

Longboards are also very vulnerable in the impact zone. They break easily in big surf because of all the torque a thundering wall of soup places along its length. Shortboards, with less length to twist and turn, seem to have less of a problem with the tumult.

Getting out is easier at reef or point breaks even when it's top-to-bottom because you can paddle around the impact zone, which is relatively stationary and predictable compared to beach breaks. However, unless you never wipe out, you will have to deal with the impact zone sooner or later.

Beginner Waves

Good waves for learning are small and mushy. You just need something strong enough to propel you along. Stay away from the top-to-bottom variety. The ideal beginner wave just sorta spills over when it breaks. They're easier

No Way: Getting out will be one trial and riding will be the next in these super hollow conditions. Top-to-bottom waves are sometimes difficult to maneuver on with a longer board and tend to break things. But see page 38!

Very Nasty: Getting out in consistently pounding beach break is sometimes impossible on a longboard.

Your Spot: For starting out, these well-shaped, hip-high little crumblers are perfect. It's an easy paddle out and there's no crowd.

**Remember:
Learning
Should Be
Fun!**
Pick your spot
and your equip-
ment with care to
ensure that you
do have fun.

Geoff "Red" Whisner just cruising in San Clemente.

to punch through, easier to catch, and they deliver a much softer blow.

Don't paddle out into the middle of the pack. If there's a crowd at a given surf spot, slink over to the side. Now is not the time to compete. You and your surfboard will part ways often during the learning process so stay away from everybody. Also, nice sandy beaches mean nice sandy bottoms. Much better to negotiate than rocks or cliffs.

Ride Time

Although shortboards provide more turning ability than longboards and as such more in the way of spectacular movement, it doesn't mean a thing if you can't catch a wave. If you're just sitting out there (and admit it shortboarders, there is alotta that isn't there?) surfing ain't much fun.

Surfers clock in an unbelievable amount of sitting time over the course of a month of sessions. Not every swell brings us consistent, speedy, well-formed waves. Most of the time and in most places, we're blessed with something less. And it's dealing with the something less that keeps shortboarders sitting and fuming and longboarders up and riding.

Shortboarders have to ask themselves if they'd rather surf less and catch fewer waves than ride a more suitable surfboard when the conditions warrant it. The pride and stubbornness of those who say *never!* is awfully limiting when you consider total ride time.

No matter what the arguments, in the end the best surfing includes the accumulation of ride after ride. If the longboard improves your wave count, so be it. I'll take that over a cold and sore butt anytime.

It's a snug fit, but, yeah, you can *definitely* get tubed with your longboard.

Chapter 3

Pre-Launch

for Beginners: Pop-Ups & Paddling

Fitness

You don't need to be a perfect biological specimen to surf but it helps if you're used to hard exercise and you show up sober. It can be a workout.

Surfing is mostly paddling, not surfing, believe it or not. Upper body strength is something you'll need and something you'll certainly attain soon enough if you stick with it. I suppose you could lift weights or something to prepare yourself, but I think just doing the real thing is the best exercise. Paddling muscles become strong paddling muscles by paddling.

Like anything totally new, the act of paddling through the surf line will be an awkward experience. And it will be exhausting. Your arms will ache, your neck well get a crick, you'll fumble and slip off the board, and the waves will throttle you until you'll feel like chucking the whole thing.

It does get better, but you *must keep trying*.

Pop-Ups

Go to the beach. Look at the surfers. See them stand up. See them *pop-UP!*

That's what you're gonna learn how to do before you get wet.

The act of standing up from a prone position on a surfboard after a surfer catches a wave is a split second thing. In the blink of an eye and in one continuous flowing movement, a surfer literally jumps to his feet.He doesn't push up to just his knees. He doesn't lift one leg before the other. He doesn't put his arms out like a tightrope walker and stick his tongue out between his teeth.

Before you can pop-up you must learn how to stand, and before you can do that you must know which foot to put forward. In your stocking feet run and slide along the kitchen floor. Which foot is forward? That's the one.

Left foot forward is called regular foot and right foot forward is called goofy foot. (Don't ask. It doesn't matter.)

The surfer's stance is feet shoulder width apart with your forward foot at about a 2 o'clock angle to your forward direction and your rear foot at a right angle to that. Face forward with your forward shoulder at around a 10 o'clock angle. Just give it a try. Chances are you'll fall right into it.

Lie stomach-down on the floor. Do a push up, sweep your legs underneath, place your feet in the surfer's stance and stand up.There is no hesitating between each step. Do it until it's one smooth movement.

There you go.

Chapter 4

Rules, Customs &Safety

It's a Jungle Out There

The lineup (that place in the water where surfers gather to catch waves) is really something of a frontier.

First of all, you're out in the water. Maybe even several hundred yards from the beach. There are no white lines or refs to guide the action and there aren't any surf patrols to police the area. No signs. No uniforms. No official authority. It's just you, the waves and all the other surfers.

Unlike almost every group activity on the shore, somehow this bobbing bunch finds a way to govern themselves without an official roadmap. It's really a very interesting social phenomenon and I'm just a tad surprised that it hasn't been featured by *PBS* or *National Geographic.*

Because for the most part our surfing society only has one rule. And for the *most* part all surfers respect it:

> *The Surfer Who Catches the Wave*
> *Closest to the Breaking Part of the Wave*
> *has Right of Wave.*

There are variations on the theme, but for the most part all law and order begins and ends here. A surfer who takes off in front of another surfer who has this right of wave is said to be cutting off, or snaking, the legal rider.

Of course, surfers aren't angels and the lineup isn't exactly a Utopia in which all surfers obey the golden rule all the time. Like I said, there are variations. And most of the variations have to do with localism.

A Surfer's Government

Every break has its local crew. These are the surfers who surf at this particular break all the time, know the others in the crew, and have a degree of wave riding skill, although it isn't necessary that they have extraordinary prowess.

The local crew has the home field advantage and the pick of the waves over the newcomer. In order to break into any spot the newcomer needs to show deference and good will towards the locals. The newcomer cannot be overly aggressive and demanding of waves. Such behavior will not be rewarded by the home town no matter what the newcomer's level of skill is. No doubt the newcomer will find himself crowded and/or heckled out of position.

Some spots have a more rigid pecking order then others and breaking in may take quite a bit of time and diplomacy. However it is my opinion that the individual newcomer can eventually break in anywhere if he tries hard enough and follows a few simple guidelines:

Be courteous. Don't take offense. Work the point or

It Must Be Saturday: In this photo the longboarder has the right of wave because he took off first and has position closer to the curl. The shortboarder has snaked him, or cut him off.

the best area for waves from the outside in. Don't paddle into the middle of the pack. Don't snake anybody, of course, and simply try to make friends. Over the course of time this will work. The biggest blunder of all is showing up with a carload of pals. Always work into a spot as an individual.

At first glance this ritual may seem somewhat trite and primitive, but keep in mind that the lineup has no police and that things really are different out there. Just because waves are free and legally belong to us all doesn't mean squat. It's the way things are until they start patrolling the surf with jet skis. And who, outside of the legal profession, wants *that*.

And also understand that the heart of localism is not petty meanness, but respect. For the surfers who came before and the sanctity of the spot itself.

Because You Ride a Longboard...

...there are special considerations you should make with your fellow non-longboard surfers.

Skilled longboarders can easily dominate a surf spot because the large planing surfaces of their boards allows them to catch waves sooner than anybody else. Longboarders can also paddle faster, sit further outside and catch waves easier than shortboarders, boogie boarders or body surfers.

And this is the rub that has created the legendary rift between longboarders and other riders, shortboarders in particular. There is nothing more annoying to a short-board surfer than a longboarder sitting outside and catching all the waves. It can happen, and most certainly does happen at those breaks with only one or two take off points.

As a longboarder you must make a decision to be either a dick or a decent surfing citizen. You can legally hog every wave in sight or reign it in a bit and let others have their turn. It boils down to an attitude. You can block out everyone else and suffer only the ugly vibe you create, or you can take your turn and build some good will. Do you want to surf in angry waters or in a friendlier place?

I've come to think that it all comes around. What you bring to the party you take back. In the end, of course, it's your call...unless you're outnumbered and/or one of those irate shortboarders paddles in and comes back out with a board three feet longer than yours.

Awareness, Intelligence & Respect

Being safe is all about being aware and intelligent. Know where you are, where everybody else is, and what the waves are doing all the time. With these things in mind you won't run into anybody, get run over, or find yourself swept into a dangerous position.

–If you're a beginner, surf the smaller, mushy stuff, wear a leash and stay away from everybody.

–Know your limitations. The ocean is a stern master.

–If you're paddling out, punch through that part of the wave *behind* the rider if you can. Don't wreck another surfer's ride just so you can avoid the white water.

–Don't take off on top of someone caught inside. Look where you're going before you commit.

–Paddling around someone to gain position on an approaching wave is more or less snaking.

–Hold on to your board in a crowd. Longboards are awfully big things to lose. If someone gets hit with one they *will* get hurt.

–Wear sunscreen.

–Show respect and good will. That's the only way it comes back.

–And...

Learn How to Swim, Jim

One of the most outstanding examples of courage and tenacity that I've ever witnessed was a certain surfer's ability to surf with an artificial leg. I was out one day and there was this guy getting most of the waves. He managed to get position on every set, or group of waves, that came in, and capture a decent ride. He wasn't particularly flashy, but he was up and riding more than the rest of us.

Later, in the parking lot I noticed he had a severe limp. Then I saw the artificial limb. Of course, I was very impressed and moved. Like alotta of us, I go through life bitching about this and that when life isn't so bad at all. Here's a guy with a chunk of plastic for a leg and *what-am-I-complaining-about?*, you know? He's got the guts to go surfing and excel with no leg, and has a smile on his face to boot.

I was inspired. And for the whole day I didn't

complain about anything.

The following week I heard he had to be hauled out of the water because he'd lost his board and didn't know how to swim.

Once again, I was very impressed, although I haven't quite figured out why. Here's someone who sets a can-do example and overcomes a huge handicap only to neglect something as basic as learning how to swim before he challenges the surf.

I can't say too much because I forgot to mention in this, *the safety chapter*, that the first thing you must learn is how to swim.

It's so basic that I forgot.

The ocean is a wonderful place to visit, but before you paddle out you gotta be able to travel on your own from point A to point B without the help of your surfboard. Something so vitally important should not be so easily forgotten.

As far as the courage to try and to keep trying, his example certainly still shines. Because many beginners are afraid of the surf and/or become discouraged with their progress.

Well, like the brave man in this story, never say die! Surfing is 95% pure fun but that other 5% builds character, if you get my drift. There will be some awful times to endure out there. When you're so cold, tired and frustrated that you'll wanna scream. But that's exactly when you must kick it in and prevail. Those small moments of victory, like when you finally make it outside after struggling for 20 minutes, are the building blocks of confidence.

You can do it.

So keep at it until you do.

After you learn how to swim.

Chapter 5

Punching Through

... And better yet, Diving Under

Taking Aim

Pointing a longboard in the right direction is very important. As you paddle out, the nose of the board must point straight into the white water. If you get caught sideways you're history.

Punching Through

It's not always easy to get out on a longboard. There's alotta board to negotiate through the white water. And longboards can be difficult to duck dive, especially in serious conditions.

Here's how ya do it:

Push-Ups

In small, mushy surf you can just paddle straight into it with your head down, or you can push up and let the wave surge beneath your body and over the board. You'll be pushed back, so it's important to start paddling as soon as possible after the collision.

Scoot`n Shoot

When the white water looms upwards to three feet in height, you can scoot back, sink the tail of your board, and with a frog kick shoot up and over, or through the surge. It's important not to grab the nose of the board when you execute, although you may be tempted in order to keep yourself from flipping over. Grabbing the tip when the soup hits will buckle your board and eventually crack it at the nose.

Slice`n Duck or Yes, Virginia, you can duck dive your longboard!

(This, by the way is somewhat historic since as far as I know instructions for the slice`n duck have never been recorded. Heck, hardly anybody even knows about it.)

Contrary to contemporary thought, a longboard can be duck dived underneath a wall of white water. And contrary to the thinking among those very few who have heard about it, you don't have to be built like King Kong to execute it. However, this technique does require practice and it's not as easy to perform as a short-boarder's duck dive.

As the surge approaches, grab the nose, tilt the board on its side underneath you, and with your weight and arms force the board underwater. As the one rail slices down, force the other down with help from your knee or foot and make like a submarine. When properly executed there's some kinda sucking action that takes place when you bring the other rail down that really takes you deep.

It works great once you get the hang of it and makes getting out on those bigger days a whole lot easier than it used to be...

Turning Turtle or Getting Absolutely Pounded

In the old days, loggers used to flip their boards over and hug them with arms and legs when the bomb hit.

Always Point into the Surf: From the moment you wade out, direct your board straight into the waves.

Push-Ups: This trick will see you through most of the little insiders.

1

2

Scoot`n Shoot:
When it gets
bigger, paddle hard
towards the soup,
scoot back, sink
your tail, and frog
kick through the
foam. Note the
proper angle of
Christine's board.
Any higher and
she flips over.

3

1

2

Slice`n Duck:
When it gets bigger yet, dive under the soup by slicing a rail and pushing down on the deck near the nose with arms and legs. See more of the slice`n duck technique on the next page.

1

Slice `n Duck in Action: Today's lighter longboards make diving alot easier than it used to be.

2

Turning Turtle: The original technique for dealing with overhead conditions. Look closely and you can see the surfer's hands gripping the board.

Needless to say, they got the crap beat outta themselves. You can still see surfers *(Wham!)* doing this one.

Another inefficient diving trick is to scramble up and hug the front of your board with your arms and *(Bam!)* legs.

As you can guess, these moves won't exactly punch you through the whitewater. Only slow down your backward progress...maybe (and punch you out for sure).

Avoidance

Your best alternative is to avoid white water paddling as much as possible. No matter what you do or how good you are at it, the ocean always wins when it's big and consistent. You get beat up and so does the board. Getting caught inside just once can sap all your strength.

Much better to understand the break you're surfing. Take the time to read the conditions. Where is it breaking? When do the sets arrive? Is there a channel or a rip or any deep water that can serve as a way out? What are the other surfers doing? How are they getting out? Are there cross currents? Like anything else, there's an easy way to learn and a hard way. Be aware and use your head *before* you commit, especially in overhead surf.

Then the secret to getting out is timing the sets and paddling hard and fast. Once you get going on a longboard they are wonderful paddling vehicles, and as stated previously, much faster than a shortboard.

It should be noted that you may not be able to get out on a big, consistent day on a longboard. And there's no shame in that.

When Bailing is the Better Part of Valor

You are responsible for your surfboard at all times. You don't want to let it go into someone, obviously. However, holding onto a longboard in the face of a mountain of white water is not an easy or healthy task. It can literally tear your limbs from their sockets.

To be sure, never paddle out directly in front of another surfer. Let there be room for the ultimate bail when you become the ultimate nail.

What Really Big Aussies Do

Bill Stewart has told me this story twice, so it must be true:

"Frank Latta and I were surfing some good size waves in Australia, maybe 10 feet, and we got caught inside. Along came this huge wall of white water and it looked like a problem. But Frank stood up on his board, sank the tail first, then the entire board, and then completely disappeared underwater(!) The soup passed him by without a scratch.

"I saw him do that all day. Sinking the board like that just wasn't a big issue for him. I imagine, though, that it does take a high degree of skill to execute, and, like anything else, alotta practice to pull off."

(Sorry, no pix of this particular feat, although I wish we did. Maybe in the reprint.)

Chapter 6

Catching Waves

The Good News

As mentioned earlier, waves are easier to catch on a longboard than on a shortboard due to their increased surface area. They pick up the swell sooner so you can sit farther out than those in the normal shortboard lineup.

Sitting and Waiting

Once you've discovered the lineup, sit up on your board and face out to sea. At this point you should be able to turn around easily and slide down to a trimmed paddling position. You must be able to execute this move in a quick, confident manner before you try to catch waves. If you're bumbling about just trying to lie down straight on your surfboard, you'll hardly be prepared to take off when the swells come marching in.

So practice. Sitting and facing one way with the nose of the board raised above the water line...then turning around 180 degrees...scooting down into a trimmed

1

2

Just Sitting, Turning Around & Paddling:

Very simple yet very important to learn before you can concentrate on catching waves. Beginners must learn to comfortably sit on their boards, turn them around at a moment's notice, and immediately paddle in trim. You don't wanna be flopping around making adjustments at this point!

3

4

paddling position... and paddling. Like the pop-ups, this movement should be one flowing thing without alotta helter-skelter adjustments.

Even if you're an accomplished shortboard surfer, it will take some practice to get a feel for the new length and width of the larger surfboard. There's just more board to turn around and control. Chances are, as a shortboarder you'll want to trim yourself too far forward* because you're not used to all that length in front of you.

Catching Soup/ for Beginners

After you think you can plop down and paddle fast enough, try catching some white water. It'll give you a feel for a speeding surfboard and a lesson in trim.

Just let the white water pick you up. Keep the nose pointed straight towards shore. Your trim should be OK if it was OK for paddling, but you'll find out soon enough.

If the surfboard pearls, or nosedives, you're too far forward. If the white water passes you by without picking you up, you're too far back. Just as in paddling, the nose of your surfboard should be just an inch or so above the water as you speed along.

If you're quick, you can adjust your trim by pushing yourself up and back on the board to raise the nose, or scooting up to push it down.

You can try popping-up at this point if you'd like. It's just bumpier in white water than on an unbroken swell. If you decide to try, don't hesitate. Pop-up in one quick movement from belly to feet.

---

* By the way, this *too far forward* stuff will echo on down the line as we get further into technique.

1

2

Catching the Swell: Christine's board is in perfect trim with the nose just clearing the surface. She's also in perfect sync with the wave. She's not too far in front of the wave or too far behind. As she picks up the wave she can comfortably begin her pop-up without any last second thrashing about.

Catching Swell/ for Beginners

Catching the unbroken peak before it spills over is the first real step for beginners and not a small deal for short-boarders who have never caught a wave on a longboard. The trick is getting into the wave soon enough, and in proper trim.

Beginners should get an idea of where the waves are breaking and paddle further out from there. It's important to get into the wave well before it curls over.

As a swell approaches, turn around, lie down and paddle towards shore. If the wave passes you by, you know to start this procedure sooner. If the wave breaks on you, or is so steep that you pitch, you know to start farther out.

When you've caught the swell properly, you'll feel the wave's energy through your surfboard. It is an unmistakable and a quite remarkable sensation (your head will buzz and the music will play). The board will become fully engaged with the swell and pick up speed right away. The nose of the board should be well above the water yet horizontal (not jutting up in the air).

You may want to stay prone to get a feel for things before you pop-up. Heck, just sailing in on your belly is a rush when you're starting out!

If you choose to stand, remember to pop-up quickly with no thought or hesitation as soon as you feel the board being picked up. You'll fall down at this point, perhaps all morning or all afternoon, but that's just part of the process. Don't be discouraged. Because sooner or later you'll pop-up and stay up. Your feet will finally know where to go and the board will do exactly what it's supposed to do.

And then you'll know...

1

2

**Catching the Swell &
Standing:** There really are no
words for the very first
time... Compare this pop-up
with the one on page 41.

3

4

This Will Happen

You'll be screaming along at 75 mph, in control with every eye on the beach on you...

Lookit that guy go!

You'll think:

WOW!

I'm standing UP!

On TOP of the water!

I'm SURFING!

We're talking moments here, but those moments will rank right up there with your first Christmas morning, first bike ride, first hit, goal or catch, first kiss, first home run (in or out of the park), first meaningful paycheck and first successful public speaking engagement.

Yup, the first time really is like that. For everybody.

Catching Swell/ for Shortboarders

If you're a shortboarder riding a longboard for the first time, you've begun to discover just how weird it is.

Man, the board's so big. It's like a boat. Getting out is a real hassle because you don't know how to duck dive it yet. And finding the trim on the thing isn't real obvious either. You're used to the nose being right under your chin, but now it's off in the distance.

Well, catching waves is a little weird, too.

Shortboarders must learn how to trim farther back then they're used to when they paddle for a wave. There is a tendency for shortboarders to trim too far forward on their longboards at first because they're not used to all that length in front. Obviously, this will cause the board to pearl.

Shortboarders must also learn to catch the swell sooner than they do on their shorter boards. Shortboarders are used to taking off when the wave is relatively steep as the smaller planing surface cannot pick up a swell until there's something to slide down. However, if a surfer waits too long to get into a swell on a longboard, too much of the board will be extended down the rapidly curving face of the wave and the nose will dig. Late take offs are possible on a longboard, but a surfer usually has to angle the drop somehow.

It's time for a tiny lesson in physics:

Glide

The key factor and physics involved with longboard take offs is glide. Shortboards don't have it but longboards most certainly do and that is one of the prime advantages of surfing a longer board. Glide enables a surfer to paddle a board faster, catch waves sooner, trim through flat sections with ease and, in general, ride more parts of a wave. What gives a surfboard glide is surface area and volume. The more you have, the greater the glide and the faster you go.

Shortboards, on the other hand, have little volume or surface area. A nine foot surfboard has about twice the volume of a modern 6 1/2 foot thruster. Shortboarders don't really paddle their boards as much as they *swim* them. They don't catch a wave as much as they *drop down* the face of one. Shortboards are useless in flat sections, mushy surf in general, and smaller waves. And they can only ride the pocket, or steepest part, of a wave. Sure a shortboard can be forced to perform in most conditions, but only with sheer paddling strength and/or alotta jumping and pumping and flicking about.

What this means to a shortboarder crossing over to longboarding:

Getting used to the trim and the take offs isn't really all that difficult. It's a matter of sitting further out in the lineup, getting back on the board, starting your take offs sooner and appreciating the gliding aspect of wave catching on a longer board.

For shortboarders this means relaxing a bit when you pick up the wave. Since you're catching the wave so much sooner than before, take offs are just a tad less critical. It's like there's another split second or two involved in the process and all you have to do is slow down and flow with it.

Pearling: Perhaps the most common error among crossover shortboarders is trimming too far forward when they paddle for waves. That, and taking off too late. In both cases the board nosedives, or pearls.

A Rather Graphic Example: Of nose navigation. From this perch a surfer sees only the rising wall of wave in front of him. Like he's surfing on just the soles of his feet.

Part Two:

The key to longboarding prowess is the cross-step.
Anything else is just stumbling.

Chapter 7

Angling&Cross-Stepping

The next trick is to angle ahead of the curl. The easiest way to do that is to take off at an angle. Even if you're an expert shortboarder you may want to just angle through a couple of waves before you start with the turns in order to get used to the longer stick as it glides down the line.

Just take off in the direction of the breaking wave. If the wave breaks from left to right, angle right. If it breaks right to left, angle left. After you pop-up, maintain the proper stance and enjoy the ride.

If you're a beginner you'll discover the difference between frontside and backside surfing if you try angling both ways, as you should. Frontside means that you and the wave face each other and backside means that your back is to the wave.

As a general rule surfers remain a little more comfortable facing the wave, however, it's not like switching stance in the batter's box or trying to write with your opposite hand. It becomes more of a preference type of thing.

Trimming

This is where longboarding becomes longboarding.

In order to keep your speeding board in proper trim you must at times pace up or back along the length of the board. To keep the nose from pearling or to slow down, you step back. To keep the board from stalling or to speed up, you step forward.

Exactly how far you advance or retreat to gain optimum trim in a given situation depends in part on your surfboard. For example, boards with a flatter rocker have different trimming requirements than a board with a kicked up nose area. A surfer must learn to read both the wave and the way his board reacts with it. It's a feel thing and it takes some getting used to.

Shortboarders will find the footwork a little awkward at first and may have a tendency to trim too far forward. Again, having four feet of board in front of you will seem real odd at first. But the results of proper footwork are so immediately obvious that getting into it will be easy. And fun.

Most surfers never learn the proper fundamentals of longboarding footwork. I didn't learn until I wrote this chapter and had the help of some great surfers who know. Like alotta guys, my footwork was some hybrid of walking, skipping and shuffling. It worked up to a point but instead of getting into that, here's how you *should* learn to trim...

Cross-Stepping

Traveling up and down your surfboard should be executed with graceful and fluid footsteps. Exactly like ballroom dancing. You don't waltz or tango with frenzied, stumbling footwork and you don't surf that way either.

It's an interesting and a rather odd mindset to have before you start surfing in the rock and roll world of

Christine angles left on her backside (back to the wave).

1

2

Brother Mike angles right on his frontside (facing the wave).

1

2

1

2

3

4

5

6

Cross-Stepping: One, two, cha, cha, cha. The footwork is more like a dance step than anything else. To do it right you gotta have rhythm and balance. Learn it so it becomes second nature.

waves, but that's exactly what fundamentally sound longboarding requires.

The basic step in our little longboarding dance is the cross-step. It's very simple and designed to provide maximum balance and control as you walk your surfboard.

From the basic upright position, or surfer's stance, bring your back foot across your front foot. As the traveling foot touches the surface, bring the other foot from the back to the front. Feet remain in the original angles (or thereabouts) of the surfer's stance throughout. That is, your feet remain at right angles to the stringer, or the length of the board. This enables the surfer to trim his edges at any time during his walk. Toes are never pointed straight ahead as they are during, say, a walk in the park.

Reverse the process to go backwards. Don't lift a foot unless the other is planted.

That's it.

It seems very simple and it is. But on a speeding surfboard you'll forget and resort to shuffling and skipping. Shuffling is jerky and skipping requires both feet leaving the surface and slamming back into it. If your stepping is jerky and bouncy, your ride will be jerky and bouncy. And out of control.

What you need to do is to train yourself to think and execute only the cross-step. That means practice. Move the furniture and cross-step in your living room until it becomes as fluid and natural as walking.

(In my living room?)

Yes! When you're up on the board and surfing you don't want to be *thinking* cross-step, you want to be *executing* cross-step. Learn how to do it now before you learn bad habits. It only makes it more difficult if you have to unlearn before you re-learn the right way.

1

2

After a turn and a nifty cut back from the back of his board, Mark Stewart shows how ya hot-foot-it to the nose...

With a cross-step, of course.

3

Although somewhat unspectacular when compared to the higher performance tricks, gracefully executed cross-stepping is one of longboarding's sweeter maneuvers.

4

Chapter 8

Turning

Cutting Back & Kicking Out

Sweetspots & Rails

To turn a longboard, the rear foot must be planted towards the base of the board. Since every board is different, it's up to you to locate the sweetspot on your board. You'll know it when you find it. The board will respond fluidly when you plant, push and turn in the direction you've decided to go.

If you're too far back the board may spin out. If you're too far forward the board will dig a rail and you'll simply tip over. The latter is the most common mistake. Shortboarders are especially prone to turn while too far forward at first for the same reason they tend to trim too far forward. They're not used to seeing all that board sticking out in front of their feet.

At this juncture it's necessary to point out the role of your longboard's edges, or rails as it relates to changing directions, or turning this way and that, during your ride:

———————————▶ *Rails Rule*

As related in the equipment chapter, longboard rails must be considered before any change of direction takes place. Unlike a shortboard, which has very little rail line, longboard rails like to set a track and stay in it. You cannot budge a longboard from its track without making some serious efforts to release it. Shortboards can be flicked about almost at will. Longboards need to be turned from the tail in big swooping arcs. Thus, a longboard surfer has to think about what he's gonna do and how he's gonna do it before he actually trys to pull it off.

When to turn is something you'll pick up as you surf more and more. Turn too soon and you may turn out of the wave. Turn too late and the curl will pass you by. Since every wave is different, the turning point(s) varies from wave to wave.

As time goes by you'll develop a feel for turning and you won't even think about it. It will become reflex. You'll learn to turn high in the wave (top turn) and low (bottom turn) depending on what the wave is doing or what you feel like doing and/or what your board is capable of.

It's easy to get locked into turning frontside because that's the favored direction of most every surfer. However, since waves break both ways it's important to feel comfortable surfing backside as well. Besides, as you learn to maneuver during the ride you'll be incorporating both frontside and backside turns no matter which way the wave is breaking.

Trimming After Turning

After you turn and you find yourself headed towards the shoulder of the wave, you may need to cross-step

Simple Turn & Trim:
After catching the swell, Christine immediately plants and pushes off her rear foot in order to swing her board right.She advances forward to gain trim and to set her inside rail in the upper third of the wave.

1

2

3

4

Cutting Back: In order to stay close to the breaking part of the wave, Ted Robinson plants his rear foot and turns back into it. Once there he makes another frontside turn.

1

2

3

More Cutting Back: This sequence clearly shows that cutting back is a matter of connecting both frontside and backside turns.

1

2

3

4

Witness: The power and grace of longboard turns. Note the foot placement. Mike's back foot is firmly planted on the sweetspot which frees the rails and enables him to make these sweeping arcs.

82

forward on your board to achieve ideal trim. Usually you do. After all, you executed the turn from the back of the board and the nose of your board may need to be lowered.

As you cross-step forward, the board will pick up speed and away you'll go. Hopefully you've dropped into a wave with an evenly cresting shoulder or section that you can race across, just ahead of the curl.

This is where you want to be during a ride no matter what you're doing. There and slotted in the upper third of the wave. Whether you're cruising, noseriding or slashing some maneuver, the ideal spot is just ahead of the breaking part of the wave and/or the upper third of the ledging swell, where the wave is steepest and fastest. Although you can venture out from these power bands with your longboard and ride other areas of a given wave (where a shortboard can't), you'll always want to come back to recharge in or near this power pocket.

Cutting Back

If your wave doesn't close out, chances are you'll speed ahead of the curl out onto the flatter section of the unbroken wave since surfboards often outrace the pace in which a wave breaks. There your surfboard will lose speed and stall. Eventually the wave will catch up, of course, but in a stalled, standing position you'll probably get clobbered.

In order to maintain speed during your ride you must position and re-position yourself in the ideal location just in front of the curl and/or the upper third of the wave. The easiest way to do this is to simply cross-step backwards on your board and slow your forward progress when you feel yourself jetting too far out ahead. As the wave catches up simply re-set the trim and increase your speed.

A much more fun and dramatic way to play with the

curl is to turn back into it with a cut back. As the wave catches up, the surfer re-positions himself and executes another forward turn to race ahead. Depending on the quality and length of the wave, this process of turning, trimming, cutting back and turning again can play itself out several times over.

A cut back is essentially a partially executed backside or frontside turn, depending on the direction of your angle. The surfer plants his rear foot upon the sweetspot at the tail of the board, pushes and turns until the board swings towards shore or at an angle towards the advancing curl. The surfer holds this course until the wave once again peaks up around him and he can execute another forward turn.

Kicking Out

Kicking out is how you exit a wave, usually to avoid a closed out section. Like cutting back, it's essentially a turn. When you wish to leave the wave, plant your rear foot and turn up and over the crest of the wave.

Don't Make Me Laugh

The first time I tried to turn a longboard, I laughed and fell off. The experience was so totally foreign after all the years I had spent shortboarding that I felt like I was surfing for the first time again.

Now this brings up two very important points:

1) You must *laugh* as you learn.

2) You *are* learning how to surf.

You gotta have fun with this. Especially you proud shortboarders. Don't get mad and pissy. Laugh it off. Longboarding and laughter just sorta fit together anyway. It's some kind of karma thing that the world of shortboarding can sometimes be short of.

And since you are re-learning or learning for the first time, relax and flow with the learning process. You're only a kook once, *so enjoy it!* When you start getting good you'll start competing with others or with yourself and your own ideas of how you should surf. And you know, so often that's just a load of crap because it makes surfing so *serious.*

Nobody expects you to be anything but a beginner when you're a beginner. So just have fun for now. There's plenty of time to be demanding and irritable later on.

1

2

Kicking Out: Again, this is really just another turning maneuver. Instead of turning back into the wave, Christine simply lets her turn take her out the back.

Connecting Turns: Ted Robinson putting it all together in a ride at the Huntington Beach Pier. In order to maintain position in or near the curl of the wave, Ted constantly changes direction.

6

7

8

9

This overview illustrates the importance of turning during the course of just one ride. Only in the fastest waves does a surfer merely angle in one direction, trim and hold steady. Most of the time you're constantly seeking the moving pocket through turns.

There is no other sport, heck, there is no other endeavor outside of a shoe salesman's dreams that places so much emphasis on feet. Ted Robinson plants a very solid looking five on the tip.

Chapter 9

Basic Noseriding

Even in Kansas City they know what *hanging ten* means.

Before shortboards took over the mantle of High Performance Surfing, the ultimate trick or maneuver in our sport was walking the length of a surfboard and riding the very tip. And although today's best longboarders can now slash about, bang the lip, ride the tube, and spin around in 360s, riding the nose is still considered to be one of the most demanding and spectacular feats in surfing.

It's like surfing without a surfboard when you're up there... in absolutely perfect trim where the curl meets the peaking swell... the most critical and powerful point of a wave. Even the hardest of the die-hard shortboarders will concede the worthiness of a gracefully executed noseride. It's beautiful to watch, difficult to do, and, of course, you can really only do it on a longboard.

It's also a very big part of our surfing heritage and, to a lesser degree, our connection to popular American

Culture. Bart Simpson, like all of those land-locked folks in Kansas, only know that surfers are the guys that... *Hang Ten, Man!*

After all, he doesn't refer to a typical shortboard maneuver, like say, *cool floater!* Or *rad roundhouse!*

Not that we need the endorsement of a cartoon character or anyone else, mind you. Or that we mean to put down shortboarding, for heaven's sake.

Noseriding is simply Classic Surfing.

And just plain fun.

Noseriding & Tipriding

The first 36 inches of a surfboard is considered the nose. Noseriding, therefore, is surfing your weight anywhere in that vicinity of the board. Tip riding is riding the tip, say the first 16 inches of the board. Tip riding includes the aforementioned hanging ten (ten toes over the nose) or a tight five (five toes over without a stretch).

Tipriding is the most challenging aspect of noseriding. It takes a great deal of practice to be able to get up there and *stay* up there for any length of time with any poise and grace.

Getting Up There

Before you just show up on the nose there's a certain amount of stage preparation that has to be done. All this prep work is called setting up. And actually, a good deal of what goes on in setting up a longboard in order to noseride is simply basic trimming procedure with a wind sprint and proper weight placement.

Once you've caught the wave and turned from the back of your longboard, it's time to head for the upper third of the wave and trim out with a cross-step. This is basically what part of the last chapter was all about.

As you're heading upwards from your turn, cross-step

1

2

Setting Up for the Tip:
You can't just run up to the nose without a calling card. The nose has to be ready for you. Mike sweeps into a bottom turn and turns up into the upper third of the wave. Note the upward angle of his board in pic #3: he has set up his board for a forward trim. He immediately and without hesitation cross-steps ALL THE WAY to the tip. How long he stays depends on the wave and board placement.

3

4

Setting Up & Tip Riding with Staying Power: With a bottom turn, proper board placement and a fast forward trim, Mike gets up on the nose quickly. He stays there because his inside rail is set into the upper portion of the most critical section of the wave and the curl has enveloped the tail of his board, thus holding it down. In the final frame, Mike has to trim back because he has surfed out of this power band. (In sequence from left to right.)

quickly up to the nose. That is, *very* quickly without hesitation. While the board is heading up it serves as an excellent platform for your forward weight placement. Then place your weight towards the inside rail (the rail riding in the wave) and... there you go.

Placing yourself over the inside rail sets the rail into the face of the wave so that it can also help support your weight. And ideally, just at this point, the breaking part of the wave will envelop the tail of your board and hold it down while you're arching on the tip.

How long you stay on the nose before you must trim backwards depends on your equipment, the wave and the way it's reacting with your surfboard. Something has to support your weight on the forward tip of the board and/or something has to hold the tail down. For the most part, it's setting the rail properly in the upper third of the wave nearest the curl that'll keep you there. Once you outrace the curl and/or begin a downward angle out of the upper third of the wave, you'll need to trim back, cut back and re-set up all over again.

On faster, or hollower waves it's possible to noseride without setting up first with a complete turn. After dropping in at an angle you can set your rail quickly with a half turn and simply make a run for the nose. All that water rushing up the face of the wave will give your board the support it needs to hold your weight up there.

'In general, in order to noseride your board you need to set the inside rail into the face of the wave, preferably in such a manner that the breaking parts of the wave hold down the tail. It's very important to cross-step quickly to the nose, preferably at that point when the board has been released from a turn or half turn and has been directed up into the upper third of the wave. Obviously, running up to the front of a surfboard while it's speeding down the face will have you hanging ten underwater.

Although the physics of noseriding are easy enough to

But I Thought I Had It: Mike takes off on a steep section and is able to advance immediately to the tip because the upward flow of water provides a very stable platform for the nose of his board. However, by the fourth frame he's dropped completely out of the power band in the upper third of the wave. Without trimming back, he pearls in the trough.

understand, actually doing it yourself will take a great deal of practice. Like everything else about this sport, it takes alotta surfing time to get the feel for what the waves are doing, what your particular board does with different waves, and what you can do to make rider, board and wave cooperate in a graceful, fluid manner.

Good Practice

According to Bill Stewart, Master Noserider, the biggest problem his students have had is committing to the nose. There is a tendency to move forward much too cautiously which throws off timing and balance. He suggests practicing the nose walk exclusively during several sessions. After the initial turn, try cross-stepping up to the nose and back continuously, without any other maneuvering, throughout the duration of your rides. Make sure you go all the way to the tip as fast as you can on your forward runs.

In fact, he learned noseriding as a boy by practicing the above... on a lake! That way he *had* to learn how to run up and back on the board quickly.

And Watch the Surfers Who Know How

This cannot be overemphasized. Watch the guys that put it all together out there. Then practice until you can do it your way.

Statement: Longboards are no longer turn & trim machines. They slice and dice, ladies and gentleman, just like their little cousin.

Chapter 10

Doing What the Pros Do

Off-the-Lips, Floaters & Helicopters

It wasn't all that long ago that longboards were simply turn and trim vehicles. Dramatic vertical maneuvering and directional change were impossible on the fat and clunky logs of yore. All that rad stuff was for shortboards only.

The advent of modern longboard design took the sport into a whole new arena of high performance. Now all these things: off-the-lips, floaters, tight tube rides, 360s, even aerials, are possible with nine feet of surfboard. As mentioned earlier, the longboard surfer must simply make special allowances for rail length and planing surface before he commits.

So much of what has been done on a shortboard can now be executed on a longboard. The only difference is feel. The fun and exhilaration of ripping it up is exactly the same.

1

2

3

4

Off-the-Lip: In the first photo, Mark Stewart coils into a bottom turn and eyes his target. The drop has given him the speed he needs to drive back up the face and meet the pitching lip of the wave with the bottom of his board. As he unweights, the lip pushes Mark around and down.

The Word From On High

For the scoop on high performance I went to the source. Bill Stewart essentially created the first long-boards capable of executing progressive maneuvers and has spent over 10 years pioneering the type of longboard surfing that now dominates the contests and premier longboarding breaks the world over. Here's Bill and the legendary Henry Ford, one of the world's finest 50 to Dead surfers, telling me all about it in between surf stories. We're at Stewart Headquarters in San Clemente, California 4-2-96:

Off-the-Lips

Doug: *I want to get into the high performance part of longboarding– those maneuvers after noseriding which represent the most extreme expressions of long-boarding. They would include off-the-lips, floaters and 360s. Let's start with off-the-lips.*

Bill: There's a weighting and unweighting technique to getting the board above the lip of the wave. It's one of the harder things for people to learn. Especially older people who don't have that light, springy feeling in their legs anymore (laughter). What it is... you compress, or coil up in a crouch during your turn off the bottom. As you come out of the bottom turn, you extend your body out and that projects the board and helps gain momentum up the face of the wave. Then you lift yourself up until you're almost weightless. You pull the board around, recoil your body, land at the bottom and take up the shock.

Doug: *Are there different types of off-the-lips?*

Bill: There's a bunch. There's a standard: you turn, go

up, have the white water hit the bottom of your board and land again. That's more of a roller coaster.

In vertical surfing, where you really want to get the board straight up and down, you shift your back foot really far back on the tail. First of all, you always put your eye ahead of what you're doing. You should surf 15 feet ahead of where you are. When you come off the bottom, you should be pinpointing where you're going to put the bottom of the board. As the lip is throwing, you throw the board up there. So you compress during the turn, then you spring out and up, and let the lip hit the bottom of the board. The lip throws the board around. You compress again, you go back down and take up the impact. That's for a serious vertical re-entry. It's not just a roller coaster, where it closes out in front of you when you're going down the line and you simply ride up on the white water and come down with it.

Hitting the white water properly also requires a certain technique. If you have all of your body weight on the board, you'll sink into the foam. You want to weight and unweight over the white water. You want to stay high on it, but keep the projection going. Like a floater. That's how they do those floaters. They're very light. They're unweighting their body across the water. Especially over the foam. If you go up with all your body weight, you'll just plow and sink. Like a water skier when the boat is moving too slow. Unweighting keeps the momentum going.

Doug: *It's the timing of the weighting and unweighting...*

Bill: Yeah. It's critical. There's a series of body movements... even Henry, who's 57 years old...

1

2

3

Totally Vert: Ted Robinson tucks into a bottom turn and takes it straight up and straight down: the ultimate off-the-lip. This sequence shows all the basic ingredients: coil at the bottom, release at the top, perfect location and timing, and board bottom flush with the lip.

101

Doug: *You're 57 years old? You don't look 57 years old!*

(Laughter)

Henry: I kept my hair.

Bill: Henry does big roller coasters. I bet he does more radical roller coasters than he ever did.

Henry: Ever did in my whole life.

Bill: Because the boards go faster. He watches other people and sees the technique. He's able to push out of his turns and he has learned to unweight his board off the top...

Henry: And use the wave's forces. In other words, sometimes you'll see a section coming and you'll want to get up and around it. You can use the wave. In the old days we couldn't. You were just stuck in a groove.

Doug: *Because back then the rails were big and fat and wouldn't let you...*

Henry: And the bottom of the boards were round which pushed alotta water. You never generated enough speed. When you did get up there, the board had its own inertia and took you out the back door. There was no way to get back down.

Bill: It would stall.

Henry: With the lighter surfboards you can get up

there and...

Bill: You can bank off the lip using the power of the lip to throw the board back towards the beach. To push it back into the direction you want to go.

Henry: You're utilizing the power of the wave.

Doug: *I need to get some speed up before I can do a vertical maneuver, right?*

Bill: You can either drive into the flats and do a bottom turn or you can do a mid-face turn and pump rail to rail, which generates quick speed. Then you compress your body and throw your weight into it, which spring-loads the board up into the lip. Then right at the top you unweight and come down with it. You re-land and drive again to beat the next section.

Henry: It's like skiing. You're pushing down to carve your edges, you're pushing down to carve your rails. You're unweighting to get the pressure off of your skis so you can make the transitional move into another turn.

Doug: *Vertical surfing on a flat-faced wave is a little less critical, right? You have more control over your directional change. Where with a more pitching wave you let the wave do all the work.*

Bill: It's the timing. It's the positioning. When you throw the board up there, you're putting the board in a position so that the power of the wave hits the bottom of the board. To surf vertically and really bash the lip, you go straight up, the bottom of the board gets hit by the lip, you turn and re-land it.

When you come off the bottom and you throw it into the lip, as the wave's pitching and the board's going up, it hits under the forward 3/4 of the board. But you can continue that line, still going straight up until the tail is just tapping the lip. Or you can get air.

Henry: But the initial collision with the lip is moving you back towards the beach a bit even though you're still going vertical. It's that BANG! that starts the whole maneuver and you have to be perfectly positioned.

Doug: *Timing with the pitching lip. With the bottom of your board facing the lip.*

Bill: If you don't get the lip to hit the bottom of your board, it'll just take the board out from under you. You have to be precisely on the opposite side of the power.

Floaters

Doug: *How about floaters?*

Bill: I think the purpose of the floater was to find another way around white water. In the 60s everybody just tilted their boards and angled and kind of slogged through the white water. Now, if you've got alot of speed going, you can weight and unweight, spring-load and jump the back of the wave. There you try to stay unweighted and as light as you can for as far as you can. When you go over and hit, you throw it into another projecting bottom turn and beat the section.

Doug: *You're actually riding the back of the wave.*

Bill: Yeah. No one knew that the back was a ridable spot on a wave. Everybody thought that you just got pitched if you ever went up there.

Henry: But the fact is that the shortest distance between the two points is not down and around the section, but up and over it...

Bill: It's a straighter line.

Henry: Once you straighten out, the further down and out in front of the wave you get, the less power you have. You're in a dead zone. Speed and power is up where the curl is. The more you go out and around it, the more speed and power you lose. You can go around it only if you have enough speed to begin with...

Bill: There's only two speeds. There's the speed of gravity and there's the speed of transferring... pulling your body up and extending it out for projected speed. Why can you go 15 miles an hour on a skateboard by zig zag turning? It's the same thing on a surfboard when you pump rail to rail. You're generating your own speed. With the right board design you can do that.

Doug: *Riding the back of a wave is different than riding any other area of a wave.*

Bill: Yeah. It's aerated. The trick to doing a floater is weighting and unweighting over the white water and trying to be as light as possible to maintain momentum.

Doug: *So it's a super unweight just before you hit the back of the wave?*

Bill: Yeah. You want to spring-load, jump and then you stay really light. You actually lower yourself to the board, but keep your weight off the board. If you keep your body stiff and straight it transfers the weight to the

Floater: The rider has jumped to the back of this cruncher and lightened the load by unweighting and riding low over the white water. As he comes down he absorbs the shock with knees bent. As you can imagine, the ankles can take a beating after a free-fall like this one.

Riding the Back of the Wave: The rider stays high and light as he "floats" over the flowing water. Note that the nose is angled slightly seaward and that the board is trimmed perfectly flat to gain as much planning efficiency as possible.

board. So you coil up as you're going down. When you hit the bottom, you're ready to spring out of your next turn.

Henry: Like when you ski the bumps. You suck your knees up to absorb it. You pull yourself off the board as you literally float across the section. You're very light up there. You can either come down with it or, if you're lucky, you can break out of it onto the shoulder.

Doug: *It's very interesting to see the guys get those long floaters. It's such a unique thing. A different kind of riding.*

Bill: When they hang it for a long time the board is not going in a straight line. It's going sideways because the water is pulling the board one way and they're trying to keep it in position. So the board is crabbing a little bit.

Doug: *Sorta like riding sidebar?*

Bill: Yeah. It's sideways. Not dead straight. You're flat on the board but the board's slightly angled because the water is hitting the sides of the fins. The board actually sideslips a bit.

Doug: *The nose angles a bit out to sea.*

Bill: Yeah. It's offset.

Doug: *Sorta like a snowboarder riding a rail.*

Bill: Not that extreme but that's the idea. And that's how they hold them for so long. When they want to get down they point the nose around and they go over.

Doug: *There must be a sweetspot up there...*

Bill: It's all technique. It's not just weight. It's raw skill, timing and technique. They're using the absolute total planning efficiency of their boards. There's no nose plow or tail stall. The board is so leveled out that there's no disruption. Tri-fins work better for me than single fins. Single fins will hang and stall. Smaller tri-fins will sideslip a little and carry with the wave.

Helicopters (360s)

Doug: *Take me through a nose 360 or helicopter maneuver.*

(Continued page 112)

1

2

3

4

Nose 360: Josh Baxter plants himself on the nose, drags a hand and spins one. In the second photo it's easy to see how the dragging hand gives the legs the leverage and power to force the fins free. Note in the final photo how Josh has trimmed back from the nose to prevent his board from pearling.

Another Nose 360: Step by step with Bill Stewart:
1) Set a high line one foot back from the nose.
2) Put both hands in the water to stop your forward motion.
3) Push hard with your back foot toward the beach.
4) Look in the direction that you're spinning.

110   *(Sequence continued next page)*

5

6

7

8

5) Keep your knees bent to take up the slack of the drop.
6) Back peddle as fast as you can to prevent pearling.
7) Wave to the crowd so they know it wasn't luck.
8) Then go into your next bottom turn.

Bill: You drop in and set up for a nose ride. Your front foot should be about one foot from the nose. Put both palms into the wave...

Doug: *And how deep?*

Bill: Up to your wrists. Pull a high line and push with your hands. Putting your hands in the face of the wave transfers the power to your back leg to break the fin free. When the fin breaks free, keep your hands in the water until the spinning of the board pulls them out naturally. So keep your hands in the wave and the board will spin around, past its halfway point, then your hands will pop free and you'll sling-shot all the way around. Then you must immediately back peddle very quickly to prevent pearling.

The trick is using your hands. Everybody thinks its done with the feet. You have no power with your legs standing on the board. You have power when you put both hands in the water and push forward and drag you hands in the water.

Doug: *It's like using the wave as leverage.*

Bill: Right. It's the only way you can sling-shot the tail around, all the way around in a propeller-type movement, to hit the face of the wave where you want it. Once it gets there the wave pushes you the rest of the way. When the board starts to rotate, you gotta look where you're going and get back off the nose. That's the hardest part. Getting back to the tail before it pearls.

Doug: *Well, it sounds like you can pull this off time and time again when I take the photos.*

Bill: Yeah, I can do that.

Henry: But he's getting a little older. We're not sure... (Much laughter.) Maybe we should get Jeff Kramer. (Jeff Kramer is one of Team Stewart's top ranked riders.)

Bill: Bring on Kramer. We'll see who's still boss.

(Hoots and laughter.)

But You Can't Do That on a Longboard! Throughout history certain images have profoundly influenced people and events. In 1992 Jeff Kramer forever changed the way we think about longboarding with this rocketing aerial. Progressive longboard design coupled with high performance talent created the new longboard revolution. The essence of that revolution was caught in this photograph. The perception of longboarding as a comical pursuit for kooks and has-beens was completely shattered and replaced with r-e-s-p-e-c-t.

Chapter 11

The Future Arrived...

yesterday...or, Try it! You'll like it!

Longboarding may have died more or less for 20 years but now it's back. Not as rumor or trend but as a reality in the lineups for keeps. Many may be surprised to learn that a full 50% of the boards made today are nine feet long or longer.

It's really not so odd. The history of longboarding is as old as the South Pacific. Literally. And the modern age of surfing was kicked off with longboards just 40 years ago. Shortboarding in all its slashing glory is only a tick in time.

All it really took was some retooling in the shaping room by a shaper or two with the balls and vision to bring the longboard up to date. The market is there and probably has been for quite some time. Alotta people wanna surf and it's the longboard that will accommodate most of them. Shortboarding will rule for the young and talented forever, but the potential to reach the greater numbers belongs to longboarding.

Longboards make learning and re-learning easier. And longboards allow surfers to surf until they die. With the new designs, a surfer can fulfill 90% of his surfing goals without ever riding a shortboard. It's a starting place and an ending place for everybody. And by no means a bad place to stay in between.

Longboards have become an important tool in every serious surfer's quiver. Longboarding expands the surfing horizon with its capacities for noseriding, flat-face surfing, trimming and stylistic flourish. Shortboards *rip the pocket*. Longboards *ride the entire wave*. Any wave.

Longboards can ride anything, anytime. The only thing that used to keep them out of the water was consistently pounding surf because no one knew how to duck dive longer boards. But with the newly developed slice `n duck technique (see page 55), a longboarder can now much better navigate the dreaded inside tumult alongside his shortboarding brethren.

So there.

The only thing standing in the way of the major boom that *will come* is popular perception and attitude. You know, that silly quirk of human nature that defines and judges without rational thought. Born out of fear and prejudice. The mindset that says longboarding is a bad thing because: *only kooks ride longboards... you can't rip on longboards... my friends don't ride longboards... Kelly Slater doesn't ride a longboard... I don't know how to ride a longboard... the magazines I read don't feature longboards...*

Well, most of that is old news: some of the world's best surfers rip on longboards, *including* Kelly Slater. By the way, his brother, Sean Slater, is one of the hottest around. And the magazines *will* feature longboarding very soon. Just ask Mr. Steve Hawk, Editor of *Surfer Magazine*.

As far as friends who don't know or the fears of those who never tried... *Wake Up!* Deal with It! For Pete's sake, *try it!* Hey, this is *surfing* we're talking about here. Not an oil spill or Mexican sewage. Longboarding is just another way to live the life we love.

Get with it and move over.

Cuz here we come.

You Can't Do That Either! Bill Stewart has led the modern longboard revolution since 1984 by redefining longboard design and longboard surfing. At 44, he's also helping to redefine surfing demographics. Once the province of our youth culture only, surfing has become the preferred pastime for a fast growing horde of mid-life crusaders for whom age limits mean absolutely nothing.

Interview:
Bill Stewart and
Henry Ford of
Stewart Surfboards

Bill Stewart is acknowledged as the creative force behind the modern longboard movement. His surfboard company, Stewart Surfboards, is the largest and most innovative longboard manufacturing/design center in the world today. His surfing empire also includes Hobie, Munoz, Herbie Fletcher and Christian Fletcher Surfboards. Top competitive surfer, master shaper and surfboard designer, internationally acclaimed artist and surfing industry leader, Bill Stewart is one of the surfing world's great visionaries. For a guy as talented and accomplished as all that, I found him to be remarkably low key and easy to talk to.

Henry Ford is a true surfing pioneer. Henry was one of the great names along the Southern California coast before the modern world of surfing exploded on the scene in the early 60s. A major surfing star in Bruce Brown's first films, Henry was hand-picked by Bruce to be the third surfer in the original movie classic, The Endless Summer. *Prior commitments kept him from taking that particular journey in 1966, but nothing ever took him out of the water or kept him from being involved in surfing's ferocious growth since then. Henry now serves as General Manager for Stewart Surfboards and is considered one of the premier over 50, or 50 to Dead surfers on the globe.*

119

This interview took place in Bill's shop in San Clemente, California in Spring, 1996. It was supposed to cover just a few questions I had about longboarding versus shortboarding, basic longboard design and longboard selection. Well, one thing led to another and I ended up with an overview of longboarding in general that should be required reading for anybody interested in the sport. I kept in the digressions because the whole thing just sorta works that way. By the way, the reason General Manager Henry Ford doesn't say much is because he was on the phone and in and out trying to run the day's business. He is not shy.

–Doug Werner

Doug: *What are your general feelings about longboarding and shortboarding?*

Bill: Shortboarding is the best surfing in the world with the highest performance. But not everyone can do it. Longboarding is universally fun for the five year old to the eighty year old. We've got that span of ages riding our longboards right now. I think that there's a window of time when shortboarding makes alotta sense, where you learn it young and take it to a certain age. But then you phase out of it. I mean, I can still shortboard but it embarrasses me because I was one of the top shortboarders not so long ago and now I'm just an average guy. Whereas on the longboard I'm still on a real high level. Even at 44.

Doug: *What are the basic elements of longboard design?*

Bill: You have your 60s classic style with 50-50 rails, single fin and real traditional styling...

Doug: *What do you mean by 50-50 rails?*

Bill: That means they meet in the middle. The foil part of the rail meets in the middle. As boards got modern the rails turned down. Originally, rails met in the middle and they slowly started foiling downward. The apex began turning downward.

Doug: *What's the deal with rails?*

Bill: Round rails hold water and edges release water. If you put hard edges around the back of the tail of the board, you're going to get that squirt feeling. That's why the boards go so fast now. Because they're planing efficiently. The boards in the old days were more rounded on the bottom and they rolled into their turns. They pushed water. They plowed it. As the board came around it was sort of at one-speed. You had to trim forward for speed. On the modern three fin longboard you can get back on the tail and pump for speed. You pump from rail to rail. You don't do that on the classic style boards.

Doug: *How about bottom design?*

Henry: That's where some of the really big changes came into it. Nowadays the bottom is almost perfectly flat, with concaves in it because you don't want any drag in the water. The less drag, the faster you go. When you had those round, 50-50 rails and those round-bottomed boards you pushed water. With the flatter bottoms and the concaves you actually rise up on top of the water. Our Hydro Hull is really getting air. It's on top of the water. Not buried in the water. You get ultimate speed.

Bill: Boards have evolved from a displacement type of

concept. For example, a sailboat has a displacement hull. But you take a speedboat or any efficiently planing hull, it gets up and planes on top of the water. So modern longboards are faster, their edges release water instead of push it, and they hold in better in the wave. They used to spin out. Now you can square off on a pretty good sized wave and just go straight up the face. It was hard to do that in the old days. The board would skip with the single fin.

Doug: *Because they had a round bottom?*

Bill: Yeah. They'd spin out. They didn't hold in like they do now.

Henry: Boards in the 90s also have curve– a natural curve in the shape.

Doug: *You're talking about the template? The outside outline?*

Henry: Yeah. The older shapes were more parallel. You had to square off your turns because that was just the natural way the board would go. Now with the curve and rocker in them, you can break it out of any line you get it into.

Bill: Originally, the shapes were very basic. There was nothing very clever about them. But over the years we've added all these parts. Like when vee shapes came out to help put the board over on the rail. And when we concaved out the fin– we started cutting off the back of the fins to make a narrower base in order to make the board looser. And double concaves that I've been doing for 15 or 16 years on all my boards. I vee it first then double concave it so it jumps from concave to concave.

Doug: *Where are these concaves?*

Bill: On either side of the stringer in front of the fins. That's where you're planing off of. Your back foot is on top of the side fin so you're riding off of those concaves.

Doug: *That helps you transfer your edges...*

Bill: The vee initiates the turn. It breaks the board over and lays it onto a concave. The concave gives you lift. You get a real spunky, light feeling on the water. It efficiently planes and lifts the surfboard. It gives it drive.

Doug: *That sounds like a terrific design.*

Bill: You would not go back. If you ever tried something like this you wouldn't go back. This board has a rail which is beveled to keep the edges from digging. I did that a long time ago. I've sold thousands and thousands of those boards to people. There are people who constantly come in to see the Hydro Hull.

Doug: *Can you turn this board farther up?*

Bill: Single fins turn further up than tri-fins. Tri-fins you tend to ride further back and plane off the tail. On single fins you can lean turn a little further up on the board. Tri-fins tend to track easier than a single fin.

Doug: *Explain tracking.*

Bill: That's when you lay a surfboard on a rail and it runs in a straight line. You'll fall if you're too far forward. Single fins have less of a tendency to do that.

Doug: *How about rocker?*

If you look at all the different boards available right now, there are a lotta choices of longboard styles. And rocker has alot to do with it. If it's heavily rockered, it takes a more aggressive style to ride it properly.

Doug: *They're slower aren't they?*

Bill: They're slower in slow surf. But they're faster going straight up and straight down. They don't have trim speed, but they have rail to rail pumping speed. So it's faster. It depends on the rider. If you put a bad rider on a rockered out board it'll be really slow because he doesn't know how to pump it. Whereas if you take someone like Jeff Kramer, or somebody who knows how to pump the board rail to rail, he'll make it fly. But it's more work. You've got that skateboard pumping action going.

Doug: *He's literally riding it like a shortboard?*

Bill: Yeah. That was my contribution to the sport. Taking my shortboarding ability along with my ability to shape shortboards and integrating it into longboard design. I look at a longboard as both a Porsche and a pickup truck. It's a pickup truck in the front and a Porsche in the back. When I'm on the back, I want to blaze. I want to hit vertical roundhouse floaters. When I'm on the front, I'm very nostalgic.. hang ten, nose 360s. Real stylish forward, but real aggressive back.

Doug: *So in a way it sort of bridges the two sports and the two eras. The 60s with the 80s and 90s.*

Bill: Right. That's what woke people up. Vertical power surfing. Not many people wanted to come back to longboarding until they saw progressive longboarding. When they saw people going fast, doing floaters and doing everything vertical they got really stoked. I mean, I'd get hoots at every break I surfed because they never saw anybody throw a longboard straight up the face, do a floater or air out and land in the flats. They never saw anybody do that.

Doug: *Then it's the design element that has christened the modern longboarding movement.*

Bill: Oh, of course. It's what re-launched it. And what's given longboarding credibility. You see, nobody wanted to be seen on a longboard because it was like you were a bald-headed fat guy hogging all the waves. That was the basic attitude of most surfers towards guys that rode longboards. But when they saw guys like Ted Robinson, Jeff Kramer, Colin McPhillips and others who really ripped, attitudes started to change. Ted Robinson, who's a 12-year veteran pro on the shortboard circuit, really blew minds. He surfs insane. You can't believe what he can do. So they all give longboarding credibility. That's where the negative attitude toward riding the longboard has backed off. Longboarding has a bit of respect now.

Doug: *All these riders, Robinson, Kramer, McPhillips... they've always ridden your longboards?*

Bill: Yeah. Ted Robinson and Colin Mcphillips are relatively new to longboarding. Jeff Kramer was one of the first progressive riders to take up the longboard at a very young age.

Doug: *And these guys are the cream of the crop. The*

only other top longboard rider I can think of that you didn't mention is Joel Tudor.

Bill: Joel's gone totally back to the 60s in his style of surfing. He's not riding as aggressively. But that's his choice. See, that's a design choice of where you want to go.

Doug: *I've heard he's surfing older boards just for the heck of it.*

Bill: He actually rides them in contests and wins alot. Because he runs up to the nose and hangs ten forever and turns around and walks the board backwards and does all these classic soul arch turns. He's graceful and it's beautiful the way he rides it. But it's not the progressive end of it. The majority of people don't want to go back to the 60s. He was never there, so it's new to him, I guess. And he's excited about it and he's great at it. The guy has incredible balance.

Doug: *The first time I ever saw him he wasn't surfing classic style. I saw him on TV surfing some contest in Pismo Beach 3 or 4 years ago. He won it doing 360s and all sorts of incredible stuff.*

Bill: Yeah. He's a really, really talented surfer.

Doug: *Who else have you sponsored?*

Bill: Dale Dobson is an incredible surfer. He's won every contest there is around. He's slipped a little over the last 5 years, but he was beautiful to watch for quite a while. He was one of those guys that really looked progressive. All these guys have ridden my boards, David

Nuhiwa, Dale Dobsen, Isreal Paskawitz, Jay Riddle, Stu Kenson... you name somebody. I've sponsored every one of them.

Doug: *Well, it sounds like you have fathered this whole movement.*

Bill: Yeah, pretty much. Along with Herbie Fletcher.

Doug: *When did you have the idea to start creating the modern longboard? Did you look at some old log one day with these big, fat rails and the giant fin and say to yourself "Hey, I bet if I put some modern design innovations into this shape I'll come up with a pretty cool thing?" What started that? Was there a moment of inspiration?*

Bill: Yeah... well... it varied. It wasn't one shot. It was an evolution. We put on the T Street longboard contest back in 1976 here in San Clemente. We all brought $5 and $10 surfboards that we bought at garage sales. We were surfing out there for five bucks, winner takes all. We had like 25, 30 guys... local guys. And they all had old long boards in their closets. And we all went out on these things. I always had one laying around and goofed around with it once and awhile. And in the competition... I was really ripping on shortboards at that time... and Rick James always made me shape round rails on boards... at the time I shaped for Rick James Surfboards...

Doug: *Rick James?*

Bill: Yeah. Rick James was never huge. He's the guy that cut off his thumb and put it in a block of resin. Greg Noll still has it...

(Much laughter)

Doug: *What? Well OK... go on...*

Bill: Anyway, around this time I started thinking... Why does a longboard have to be shaped so much different than a shortboard? Why take all the planing efficiency out of it? I didn't understand. Rick made a classic. He really kicked the tails alot. He put really round rails on them. The nose worked great but none of them had any speed. You could never pump them and get any drive out of them. So I went to work over at Hobie after that and made the first three fin longboard. It must have been about 3 years later that I made the short side fins. The 3 1/4 inch side fins with the 6 inch back fin and did the double concave bottom. That was about 1984.

Doug: *How about the rails? Were they still fat and round?*

Bill: No. I down railed them. I made the board really lightweight, too. I was doing two nose 360s and huge floaters...

Doug: *So it was around 1976?*

Bill: That's when it started evolving and we started thinking in those terms. Probably in the early 80s is when people jumped on it... really started to push it more progressive. I have the original short side fin board that I made. It's hanging on the ceiling in the showroom.

Doug: *Those are the fins that you can pop in and out?*

Bill: Yeah. That's a mold and template of the original.

Doug: *So you invented that?*

Bill: Yeah. That set-up is my fin configuration. It's documented in *Essential Surfing* and *Surfer Magazine*.

Doug: *What I wanted to do here was break it all down. People come into a shop these days and there's so much to choose from. They don't understand what all the design differences mean. Boards are all different shapes, sizes and fin configurations...*

Bill: I would break it into four categories. You have your classic 60s style board, such as the Phil Edwards Model. Then you have a hybrid. Some have single fins, some have three fins, but they all have downed-edges...

Doug: *With a medium rocker...*

Bill: Kind of a flat rocker. Then it goes into a more progressive...

Henry: The Hydro Hull kinda thing...

Bill: Yeah. The progressive end which started this whole thing. And then there's a pro level board, which I pull alot of people away from unless they're qualified to buy into that. They better be able to surf.

Henry: You have to be prepared to work on riding that board. You have to...

Doug: *Just like a shortboarder has to work his...*

Henry: It's like a long shortboard...

Doug: *So basically we have four categories. The traditional 60s style, and then the three levels of progressive boards...*

Bill: Yeah. And those boards are really a decision on how you want to ride and what level you're at. You know, style and level. Because you can take a guy like Joel Tudor who takes that 60s board out and wants to ride that. And there's alot of guys that just want to be seen with a 60s board. They want to relive the past. They just want to cruise and trim. Some boards you walk forward on because they have the speed spot forward of center. They're designed that way. The actual straight part of the board is forward. You walk up there and it goes fast. On the other hand, you have the Jeff Kramer Model, the LSP. If you walk forward on that board it decelerates.

Doug: *Because of the rocker...*

Bill: The nose is so kicked and concave that it plows. It's made for vertical surfing: straight up and straight down. For that you need nose rocker or you'll pearl. You take a nine foot board and it's like putting a quarter in a nickel slot. You go straight vertical like this and you come down, it doesn't fit. So you gotta kick back on the tail so it'll be able to land.

Doug: *So if a surfer is trying to find a board that'll work for him he should come into a shop like this with an honest appraisal of his own ability and find experts like you two gentlemen who will really listen and accommodate their specific needs.*

Bill: Right.

Doug: *So it's personal attention and honesty. You're servicing the client. You can almost forget the categories. I mean, they're good up to a point, but what it really comes down to is personal preference.*

Bill: Right. That's it. Here at Stewart we have 15 different demos they can try out. That really helps.

Henry: We ask the people what they want to do. Some people come in here and say, "You know, I really just want to ride the nose more. I just want to make that turn and I want to develop that part of my surfing." Then we'll lean him in degrees towards the Porky Pig, because it has a little bit bigger nose. Or we'll get a guy who says, "I never get off the tail." We'll lean him towards a Hydro Hull or towards a Kramer Model. We build boards in degrees to accommodate every surfer and every surfing condition.

Bill: Also the glass jobs come lighter and thinner at the pro level. Some guys want a 60s board with a durable glass job that will never break or dent. We make those for people. If you take the fat out of the board, the reaction time gets better. It's not body weight, it's swing weight. When you snap back, having a light board makes a huge difference. But you don't get that lightweight board unless you want to surf at that level and you're willing to pay the price. And there is a price, as you know (referring to my breaking three boards in 12 months).

(Much laughter)

Henry: You can get a 50-50 guarantee. We guarantee

you on both pieces.

(More laughter)

Bill: There is a way to glass them to make them lighter and stronger.

Doug: *Well, maybe I'll be riding a Stewart in the next month or two.*

Bill & Henry: You better be.

(Laughter)

Doug: *I guess so. Bill threatened to horsewhip me during our first phone conversation because I said I'd never been in his shop.*

(More laughter)

Henry: You know what the bottom line is here? It's authentic here. Everybody here surfs. We care. And we want people to have fun. The last word here is fun.

Doug: *Maybe that's what's missing in certain short-board circles. You know, you paddle out there and nobody smiles. Everything is sorta heavy.*

Bill: Surfing shouldn't be an anger sport. There's nothing angry about it. The hoots and the high fives with your pals on a perfect day... that's the pleasure of surfing.

Doug: *Describe a good basic start-up longboard.*

Bill: I would highly recommend that they go with what we call a trim rocker. It's a trim style board and they're straighter. I have blanks made up with different rockers. A trim rocker makes a straighter, broader entry. You want a softer rail and probably a single fin or a three fin...

Doug: *Basically the rocker is straighter?*

Bill: The whole board is wider, thicker and flatter.

Doug: *How about a shortboarder? An average short-boarder who's going to get his first longboard.*

Bill: The majority of shortboarders are average or below. There's a 1% pro level and it breaks down from there. Anybody who's a decent shortboarder should test ride a three fin longboard because they're gonna wanna go fast. They're used to going fast and turning quick. The only way you're going to get that feeling out of a long-board is with double concaves, and/or turned down rails with three fins. You need something that's going to go rail to rail real fast.

Doug: *And that swings around quickly?*

Bill: You want to know that it reacts quickly. More like the pro level board. Because they're used to the short-board paddling. When they get on a big board it paddles like a rocket ship. The dilemma for those guys is they want to turn too far forward on the board. They don't step back on the sweetspot. It's hard to get them back there.

Doug: *I think that's the biggest problem for a short-*

boarder getting into longboarding. They're used to the nose being right under their chin when they paddle, and just 2 or 3 feet in front of them when they ride.

Bill: Here's what I tell them: Regardless of the length of the board, your feet are always in the same spot when you turn on the tail. All the length goes in front of you. None goes behind you. I'm turning with my back foot in the same spot no matter what length of board I'm riding.

Doug: *It's really just getting used to all that length. I hadn't been on a longboard in 25 years and two years ago I thought I'd give it a try after riding nothing but a shortboard for all that time. I remember taking off and it looked like there was 50 feet of board in front of me!*

(Laughter)

Bill: It's intimidating for a shortboard guy...

Doug: *It's embarrassing because you run up and try to turn in the middle of the board and you dig a rail and fall over.*

(Laughter)

Bill: That's tracking. We talked about that earlier. Digging your rail is tracking. Tracking is when you load too much rail for the speed you're going. If you drop straight in, too far forward, the board won't turn because you're loading too much weight on a rail. The board will run in a straight line. If you try to turn, it'll dig a rail and you'll fall off. It doesn't want to turn.

Doug: *So you need to be farther back where there's more curve. On the tail.*

Bill: You're freeing your edges. You're reducing your rail line in the water.

Doug: *You have to think about your rails.*

Bill: That's right. You have to think about your edges.

Doug: *That's alot like skiing or snowboarding, especially. You have to think about your edges. Because you can't turn a snowboard like you can a shortboard. A shortboard you can whip around almost at will.*

Bill: That's because you're tail riding and the front end's free.

Doug: *But with a longboard you've got all that rail. You've got to know where your rail is and you have to work with the surfboard.*

Bill: You utilize your rails.

Doug: *I've heard it said that longboarding improves your surfing because you have to think about what you're doing... think about your board and how it's going to work with the wave.*

Bill: Yeah. It's true.

Doug: *So longboarding has its own challenge.*

Bill: To set up and position your board takes more

forethought. You don't just *fling* it into position. You *swing* it into position. It's not quite as reactive. So it's not like a shortboard where you just decide to go somewhere and BAM! you're there. A longboard's a little more graceful and sweeping. That's where the style of longboarding comes in. The big word is style. That's grace and form. No different than dancing or figure skating. Where the person's got style. In shortboarding, rad is important. In longboarding it's style.

Glossary

360- An advanced maneuver where a surfer spins his surfboard completely around during a ride.

Angle- A surfer's direction away from the breaking part of the wave.

Backside- When a surfer rides with his back to the wave.

Bailing- A method of dealing with an onrushing broken wave where the surfer dives underwater away from his surfboard.

Beach Break- A type of surf area where waves form over sand bars.

Bottom Turn- Turning a surfboard after the board has slid down the face of a wave.

Classic- A cool thing that has historical precedence.

Close Out- A wave without a peeling breaking pattern. A wave that breaks all at once along its length.

Consistent- A type of surf condition when waves break continuously with little interruption.

Cross-Stepping- The proper way to walk a longboard in order to achieve trim. Feet are at right angles to the board's length.

Curl- That part of a wave where the breaking part meets the unbroken part.

Cut Back- A surfing maneuver where the rider reverses his forward progress on a wave in order to reposition himself closer to the pocket or breaking part of the wave.

Cutting Off- The act of catching a wave in front of another surfer who is closer to the breaking part of a wave. Also called snaking.

Dig a Rail- When a surfer loads too much weight, too far forward on a side, or rail, of the surfboard as he rides. The board sets a track and the surfer usually falls over. Also called tracking.

Duck Dive- Thrusting a surfboard underneath the water with arms and legs in order to dive under a broken wave.

Dude- In order of historical usage: 1) A cowboy's disparaging term for a greenhorn. 2) A jazz musician's term for a guy. 3) A surfer's (circa 1972) term for a guy. 4) A mall rat's (present day) term for a guy. 5) An upper middle class white person's (present day) term for a guy. At this rate, by the year 2003 the term *dude* will become the proper term to describe a guy in the English language. It will replace: sir, gentleman, man, and fellow. As in *Dear Dude...*

Flats- That part of a wave away from the breaking and steepest part. The shoulder.

Floater- An advanced maneuver where a surfer rides the back of a broken wave.

Foam Core- The urethane blank that is shaped and encased in fiberglass and resin to make a surfboard.

Frontside- When a surfer rides facing the wave.

Hanging Five- Riding a surfboard with one foot, or five toes, placed over the nose.

Hanging Ten- Riding a surfboard with all ten toes placed over the nose.

Hard Edge- A rail shape that foils down from the deck to meet a flat bottom on a surfboard.

Helicopter- An advanced maneuver where a surfer spins his board all the way around from the nose. Also called a nose 360.

Glide- A physical attribute of longboards due to surface area and volume. Usually refers to a longboard's capacity to paddle, catch waves and ride flat parts of a wave.

Goofy Foot- Right foot forward on a surfboard.

Impact Zone- Where waves break.

Kick Out- When a surfer exits a wave by turning the surfboard up and over the wave's crest.

Kook- A beginning or extremely awkward surfer.

Lines- Refers to the lines of advancing swell.

Lineup- Where the waves begin to break and surfers position themselves to catch waves.

Lip- The tip of a breaking wave as it pitches forward.

Localism- The type of surfing behavior exhibited by local surfers. Usually hostile to visitors.

Log- Old, beat-up, and/or poorly shaped longboard.

Longboard- A surfboard usually nine feet long or longer.

Mush- Usually windblown, softly breaking waves.

Mushburger- A type of wave that breaks softly and slowly down its face.

Nose 360- An advanced maneuver where a surfer spins his board all the way around from the nose. Also called a helicopter.

Noseriding- Surfing upon the first 36 inches of a surfboard.

Outline- Looking at the deck or bottom of a surfboard, the outside shape of the entire board.

Pack- The crowd of surfers in a lineup at a surf spot.

Peak- The rearing, steep part of a wave about to break. Also that area of a surf spot where the waves begin to peak.

Pearl- When a thrusting surfboard nosedives underwater usually due to too much forward trim.

Pocket- The steepest area of a wave next to the breaking part.

Point Break- A type of surf area where waves form around and over a point of land.

Pop-Up- The way a surfer properly stands up on a surfboard from a prone position to a standing position.

Push-Up- A method of punching through a broken wave on a longboard where the surfer pushes up from the surfboard and lets the white water flow underneath the body.

Quiver- Refers to a surfer's collection of various shaped and sized surfboards. Much like a golfer's set of clubs.

Rad- Refers to a surfer's outstanding ability to skillfully surf a wave. Usually refers to a shortboarder's ability to ride up and down, back and forth on a wave.

Rail Line- The length of edge, or rail, up and down a surfboard.

Rails- The edges of a surfboard.

Reef Break- A type of surf area where waves form over rock or coral reefs.

Regular Foot- Left foot forward on a surfboard.

Rip- Refers to a surfer's ability to skillfully maneuver a surfboard around, in or under the breaking part of the wave.

Rocker- Looking at the side of a surfboard, the bend of a surfboard along its length.

S Stroke- A swimmer's stroke used by paddling surfers.

Scoot `n Shoot- A method of punching through a broken wave on a longboard where the surfer scoots back on his board, sinks the tail, and shoots through or over the white water with a swimmer's frog kick.

Section- A part or an area of a wave.

Set- The way waves arrive in a timely manner at the beach. A group of waves.

Setting Up- The maneuvering of a longboard that involves turning, rail placement in the upper third of a wave's face, and trimming to achieve ideal balance and thrust.

Shallows- The shallow water next to a coast.

Shaper- A surfboard designer and craftsman.

Shortboard- A surfboard under eight feet in length.

Shoulder- That part of a wave away from the breaking part. The flats.

Stick- A surfboard.

Slice`n Duck- A method of diving under a broken wave on a longboard where the surfer slices one rail downward, then submerges the other in order to shoot underwater and under the white water.

Slot- The steepest part of a wave. Also called the pocket.

Snaking- The act of catching a wave in front of another surfer who is closer to the breaking part of a wave. Also called cutting off.

Soup- The broken part of a wave. The white water.

Stringer- The wooden strip that reinforces the foam core of a surfboard.

Surfer's Stance- The proper foot and body position of a standing rider.

Swell- The windborn energy that translates itself into marching lines on the ocean's surface and, when it reaches the shallows, waves.

Take Off- The act of catching a wave.

Tipriding- Surfing on the first 16 inches, or very tip, of a surfboard.

Top-to-Bottom- A type of wave which pitches forward and all the way down to its base. Also called a tube or barrel.

Top Turn- Turning a surfboard at the top of the wave. Pivot turn.

Tracking- Digging a rail. The result of loading too much weight, too far forward on one side of the surfboard. The rail usually sets a course, or track, different than the surfer's intention and the surfer falls over.

Tri-Fin- A three fin configuration.

Trimming- The act of balancing one's weight on a surfboard, while either paddling or surfing, in such a manner that the board achieves maximum thrust.

Tube- A type of wave that pitches out and all the way down, and around, to form a hollow wall.

Turning Radius- The term used to connote the space a surfboard uses to complete a change of direction or turn.

Turning Turtle- A method of dealing with an onrushing broken wave where the surfer turns the board over and hugs it with arms and legs.

Wax- A traction aid rubbed onto the deck of a surfboard.
Wetsuit- A neoprene outfit worn by surfers that heats water trapped next to the skin.
White Water- The broken part of a wave.
Wipe Out- A trick we all get good at.

Stewart Surfboards:
Carving Out the Future of Longboard Surfing

Bill Stewart: World Class surfer, both shortboard and longboard. World renowned surfboard craftsman, with over 20 years of shaping experience. Nationally acclaimed artist and designer. *Man on a mission:* The creative mind and lifeforce behind the modern longboard movement.

Team Stewart, Ranked #1 PLA: Jeff Kramer, Colin McPhillips, Ted Robinson, Geoff Moysa, and John Moritz.

Legendary Craftsmen: Among the world's finest shapers and glassers: In addition to Bill Stewart: Terry Martin, Bill Shrosbree, Jeff Widener, Jerry O'Keefe, Geoff Logan, Mickey Munoz, Phil Edwards and Ron House.

Stewart Surfboards
2102 South El Camino Real
San Clemente, CA 92672
Retail: 714-492-1085
Fax: 714-492-2344

Resources

Surf Shops

The best source for practically everything is the surf shop. Surf shops have traditionally been rather small, privately owned enterprises run by surfers and probably always will be. There is no real competition from the Wal-Marts of the world and the concept of chains hasn't caught on in any big way. They are universally located at or near popular surf spots along any stretch of coast and it is there you will find the best local information about:

– Surfing Areas
– Surf Camps
– Surf Schools or Lessons
– Conditions
– Contests
– Museums
– Organizations

Shops also provide:

– Surfboards
– Surfing Gear
– Surfers to Talk to
– Surfing Magazines and Newspapers

Most shops have longboards and people hip to long-boarding so it's safe to enter. In fact, any serious shop these days caters to the longboarding market. If they don't they're missing a full 50% of their potential buyers.

Surfing Magazines

The magazines in our sport have always played a very large role.They've served as *the* forum for surfing issues, *the* showcase for new talent and hot surfing spots, *the* source for surfing information, and perhaps most importantly, *the* source for stoke and inspiration when the sun goes down and/or the surf is flat.

For longboarders:
The Surfers Journal
1010 Calle Cordillera
Suite 102
San Clemente, CA 92673
714-361-0331
Fax 714-361-2417

Longboard Magazine
110 East Palizada
Suite 301
San Clemente, CA 92672
800-284-1864
Fax 714-366-8280

Mostly shortboarding for now, but soon to be for all:
Surfer Magazine
33046 Calle Aviador
San Juan Capistrano, CA 92675
714-496-5922
Fax 714-496-7849

Surfing Magazine
950 Calle Amanecer
Suite C
San Clemente,CA 92673
714-492-7873
Fax 714-498-6485

Sources for Surfing Books, Videos, &...

Larry Block Enterprises
PO Box 3483
Chatsworth, CA 91313
1-818-340-6019
Fax 805-526-3680

Doctor Ding Surf Products
16390 Pacific Coast Highway
Suite B-9
Huntington Beach, CA 92649
310-592-9442

Mountain & Sea Publishing
Bank Wright
PO Box 126
Redondo Beach, CA 90277
310-379-9321

Surf Direct
PO Box 1965
Laguna Beach, CA 92651
1-800-506-SURF
Fax 714-494-7195

Television

Check your local listings for surf contests and surfing programs.

Videos

Check out your local video store for surfing videos. You will find them for certain in stores located around surfing areas.

Movies

Bruce Brown's *Endless Summer* and *Endless Summer II* are the ones.

The first one came out in 1966 and to this day still manages to convey the real spirit of surfing. It can be said that this movie converted a generation. Strictly longboard surfing. Classic style.

The sequel was released in 1994 and is hot not only because it also works the same magic, but features the modern longboarding theatrics of one Robert Wingnut Weaver.

Museums

California Surf Museum
308 North Pacific Street
Oceanside, CA 92054

Ventura Surf Shop
88 Thompson Blvd.
Ventura, CA 93001
805-643-1061

Hobie Sports
248 Del Prado
Dana Point, CA

Huntington Beach International Surfing Museum
411 Olive Street
Huntington Beach, CA

Santa Cruz Surfing Museum
Lighthouse Point
West Cliff Drive
Santa Cruz, CA 95062

Surfing Heritage
218 Pacific Street
Morro Bay, CA

Professional Longboard Association
217 11th Street
Huntington Beach, CA 92648
714-960-7249
Fax 714-960-7249

Bibliography

Kampion, Drew. *The Book of Waves.* Santa Barbara, Calif.:Arpel Graphics, Inc., and Surfer Publications, 1989

Surfer Magazine. San Juan Capistrano, Calif.: Surfer Publications, Inc.

Surfing Magazine. San Clemente, Calif.:Western Empire Publications, Inc.

Klein, H.Arthur. *Surfing.* New York: J.B. Lippincott Company, 1965

Index

More Start-Up Sports:

Surfer's Start-Up
Snowboarder's Start-Up
Sailor's Start-Up
In-Line Skater's Start-Up
Bowler's Start-Up

Each book in the *Start-Up Sport Series* is an ultra-readable, photo-laden guide designed to celebrate the challenge of learning a new sport with an emphasis on basic technique, safety and fun.

Start-Up guides are endorsed and acclaimed by industry insiders as well as national publications including:

Surfer Magazine, Transworld Snowboarding Magazine, Skiing Magazine, Snow Country Magazine, Outside Kids Magazine, Boys Life Magazine, The San Francisco Examiner, The Orange County Register, The San Diego Union Tribune, The Los Angeles Daily News, The Library Journal, Booklist, Small Press Magazine, The Book Reader, Action Sports Retailer Newsmagazine, InLine Magazine, Global Skate Magazine, Bowlers Journal, In-Line Retailer & Industry News

To Order Call 619-476-7125
or fax 619-476-8173
or write to:
Tracks Publishing
140 Brightwood Avenue
Chula Vista, California 91910

Books are $9.95 each, plus $3.00 shipping. Add 50 cents for each additional book. Californians add 7% sales tax.

All *Start-Up Sports* books are available in most major bookstores and sporting goods outlets nationwide.

One's Big & One's Little...

Longboarding	Shortboarding
Born a Very Long Time Ago	Born around 1967
Born in the South Pacific	Born in Southern California
Large Sweeping Radius	Tight Whipping Radius
Wave Riding	Pocket Riding
Noseriding	No way
Now it's Vertical, too	Vertical Extremus Maximus
Made to Paddle	Paddle/Swimming
Tricky When Late	Made for Pits
Gliding Entry	Free Fall
Trimming	Weight Shifts
$350-600 Plus	$250-400 Plus
Slice`n Duck	Duck Dive
Laughter	Intensity
Age 8 to Daisies (Easy)	8 to 40 (If you're Special)
Cool Designs	Cool Designs
Tubes? Sure.	Made for Barrels
Mush Gliding	Mush Pumping
Style	Rad
Float	Sink
Classic Cool	Always Hip
Historic	Modern
Stars	Super Stars
Edges, Edges, Edges	No Matter
Cross-Step	Pump
Big	Small
Paddling Velocity	Paddling Sprint
Lineup Out	Lineup In
Accommodating	Cocky
Hang Ten	360 Aerial
Set Up	React
Flowing	Ripping
Foundation	Outer Limits
Back for Good	Move Over
Great Surfing	The Best Surfing
The Book	The Headlines
52%	48%
Surfing	Surfing

About the Author

Doug Werner has been surfing since 1966. He still surfs everyday somewhere south of San Diego, California and plans to do so until he's buried or captured.Since graduating from Cal State Long Beach, he has built a graphics business, formed an ad agency, written six books and founded Tracks Publishing in 1994. All of these endeavors have been successful ploys to avoid Corporate America, coat and tie, middle ageism and most of your typical middle class responsibilities. He lives with his wife Kathleen in Chula Vista, California who doesn't seem to mind his youthful habits and somewhat bent way of thinking.

Stewart Surfboards:
Birthplace and Capital of the Modern Longboard Nation:

In 1982, when surfing was all but synonymous with shortboarding, Bill Stewart created the first modern longboard. Besides being able to noseride, it turned, burned, floated, bashed the lip and in general did all those things that couldn't/shouldn't be done on a nine foot surfboard. The Modern Longboard Nation was born.

Today nearly 60% of the boards being made are longboards. Stewart Surfboards is the world's largest and most innovative longboard manufacturing/design center in the Universe. Stewart Longboards are hand-crafted, custom-built masterpieces created by the surfing world's greatest names: Terry Martin, Bill Shrosbree, Jeff Widener, Jerry O'Keefe, Geoff Logan, Mickey Munoz, Phil Edwards, and Ron House.

Stewart Surfboards
2102 South El Camino Real
San Clemente, CA 92672
Retail: 714-492-1085
Fax: 714-492-2344

160